CW01664332

THE BATTLE OF THE *Coral Sea*

SEA BATTLES IN CLOSE UP • 12

THE BATTLE OF THE *Coral Sea*

Bernard A. Millot

Translated by S. V. Whitley

LONDON

IAN ALLAN LTD

First published 1974

ISBN 0 7110 0540 0

All rights reserved. No part of this book may be reproduced or transmitted in any form or by any means, electronic or mechanical, including photocopying, recording or by any information storage and retrieval system, without permission from the Publisher in writing.

© Bernard Millot, 1974

Published by Ian Allan Ltd, Shepperton, Surrey,
and printed in the United Kingdom by
Morrison & Gibb Ltd, London and Edinburgh

Contents

	Introduction	7
1	The forces taking part and their intentions	11
2	Preliminary skirmishes – May 7, 1942	41
3	The Battle of May 8 and its consequences	80
4	An analysis of equipment and technology	119
	Mitsubishi A6M *Zero*	121
	Aichi 99 *Val*	126
	Nakajima 97 B5N *Kate*	130
	Grumman F4F Wildcat	134
	Douglas SBD Dauntless	138
	Douglas TBD 1 Devastator	141
	Kawanishi 97 H6K *Mavis*	144
	Appendices	
1	Table showing organisation and composition of the Japanese Naval and Air resources	150
2	Table showing organisation and composition of the American Naval and Air resources	155
3	Overall American and Japanese losses	160
	Bibliography	161
	Index	163

Introduction

To judge from the many and various publications relating to the Second World War, it would appear that the conflict in the Pacific is still represented in many minds by a small number of key events such as Pearl Harbor, Midway, Leyte, Okinawa and the atomic bomb dropped on Hiroshima. It is true of course that this view is not inaccurate, but it obscures several other encounters which, although less famous and spectacular, are nonetheless significant and pregnant with consequences. The battle of the Coral Sea in particular has not always been awarded its due place in works covering the war in the Pacific, although, despite the fact that this naval air arm engagement was less decisive than those listed above, it does have a great deal of significance and, we would venture to add, was indicative of the subsequent course of events. It may even be regarded as secondary when compared with the battles of Midway or Leyte, but it is important for several reasons in the light of which it deserves to be examined.

The battle of the Coral Sea called the first successful halt to the vast military expansion of the Japanese. It was, too, the prototype of a new kind of battle, inasmuch as it marked the realisation by the Japanese of both the extent of their adversaries' potential and the limits of their own. Owing to its extraordinary nature and outcome, this event was not only to have a considerable effect on the future as the fore-runner of all subsequent naval air arm engagements in the Pacific, but was also to lend them an inherent and specific aspect which had until then remained out of focus.

Apart from these two questions, the battle of the Coral Sea, its outcome and its results gave an invaluable psychological stimulus to the Allies and at the same time delivered a blow to Japanese pride. The former realised that the hour of victory was at hand; the latter that their frenzied hegemony must have its limits. For these reasons alone, this encounter in the Coral Sea would deserve greater study, but its interest goes even further, and indeed the lessons to be learned from the battle, together with its more remote consequences, go well beyond its political, technical and psychological aspects.

On the strategic plane, it is certain that without this battle or rather without the conclusions to be drawn from it at the time, the course of subsequent operations would have been very different. Had the Japanese conquered the southern coast of New Guinea as they intended, the northern provinces of Australia would have been open to invasion, or at any rate to devastation by Japanese aircraft. This would have put paid to the role of Australia as an arsenal and a spring-board for subsequent Allied victories. The Australian Dominion might well have sued for a separate peace, as the Japanese warlords were hoping. Had the battle of the Coral Sea not occurred or had Japan had a total victory, it is therefore indisputable that the Allies, without any control over Australia, would have seen the course and duration of the Pacific War completely reversed and perhaps even transformed beyond all recognition.

On the tactical plane, this battle, which, as we shall see, had an inconclusive outcome, was bound to be one of the most instructive, since it served as an Allied criterion for new techniques, the initial effects of which were to be felt in what proved to be the very near future. Like most specialists in this field, I consider that, without the battle of the Coral Sea, Midway, which took place less than a month later, would not have been the resounding and decisive American victory that it was. Lastly another, not insignificant aspect of the Coral Sea engagement lies in the fact that it marked (a) the first Allied reaction of any importance since the commencement of hostilities, and (b) an entirely new type of battle which took place 'below the horizon', for at no point did the opposing vessels sight one another, but acted solely through the agency of the aircraft they carried. This was a technical aspect which was, I would stress, to give the Pacific conflict its unique character, since its consequences decisively contributed to the decline of battleships as capital ships in favour of aircraft carriers which were superior when used in squadrons.

These many arguments give a legitimate significance to the battle of the Coral Sea and help to restore it to its due place in the history of the Pacific War. I propose therefore to review the military situation both before and during the battle, and to end my study with a short chapter on its technical aspects which are essential for a complete understanding of the key events and factors which culminated in the battle.

B. A. M.

CHAPTER ONE

The forces taking part and their intentions

The Allies and the General Situation

A short official communiqué, issued on the very first day following the event, produced, despite its laconic phrasing, a lively and agreeable response in the United States. Although covering the battle only in part and although incomplete, the information contained in this communiqué was the first good news of any significance to reach the Allied countries at a time when they had received nothing but bad news from the Far East ever since the beginning of hostilities. The communiqué was encouraging and restored the morale of the American people who were aghast at the disastrous turn events had taken in the Pacific. It was the first light at the end of a long tunnel.

Since Pearl Harbor on December 7, 1941, the American Press had recorded a devastating progression of defeats and humiliations in the Far East. Nothing seemed of any avail in warding off the Japanese tidal wave bearing down on Eastern Asia. It is of course true that the battle of the Coral Sea was not the first Allied reaction, but it did have a new and unexpected character, and it took on a particular significance. After the disastrous outcome of the first naval engagement in the Java Sea at the end of February 1942, when the Allies yielded the East Indian Archipelago to the Japanese, the Western Powers had carried out combined air and naval assaults and reprisals on positions held by the Japanese on the Islands of the Central Pacific. These minor operations had also been designed to restore morale in both the fighting services and the United States population at home. They were also intended to bring the air and naval forces up to operational standard and, incidentally, to wreak irreparable havoc on the enemy. Then, on April 18, there had been the famous raids on Tokyo and several other large Japanese towns by Lieutenant Colonel J. H. Doolittle. These actions were of great psychological benefit, but they were unilateral in that, on the one hand, they were limited as regards the methods used and, on the other, that they produced no reaction on the part of the enemy.

The announcement of the happy outcome of the battle of the Coral Sea thus had particular significance, being evidence, both symbolic and encouraging, of an important confrontation, in a bilateral struggle which, unlike every other engagement since the outbreak of the Japanese War, had not been in vain. In fact, this battle also had other effects, but we must not anticipate.

Now obviously, no event is of any significance unless its causes are known. We must therefore examine the strategic pattern obtaining at that time in order to identify the battle more specifically in relation to time and space. The military situation of the Allies in the Far East in the early spring of 1942 was, quite simply, abysmal, and had been the result of an uninterrupted succession of reverses or defeats throughout the five months of hostilities.

The great Japanese military advances

In pursuit of a long dreamed of and meticulously planned ascendancy, the Empire of the Rising Sun had begun hostilities against the Western Powers who had colonised or taken under their protection most of the territories coveted by the Japanese. The war had started with their surprise attack on December 7, 1941, on the great American combined air and naval base at Pearl Harbor (in the Hawaiian Archipelago); it had continued with a series of almost simultaneous landings at various points in Eastern Asia and the Central Pacific. Spurred on by an apparently irresistible force and motivated by an extraordinary patriotic fervour, the Japanese armies in record time overran vast areas which one after the other succumbed. By waging war simultaneously on the United States, Great Britain and the Netherlands, Japan presented to the Western Powers a challenge which the latter, already engaged as two of them were with the war in Europe, were in no position to oppose.

The power and ferocity of the Japanese onslaught took the whole world by surprise and rapidly placed the Western nations involved in a predicament which was as disadvantageous as it was dramatic. No one had taken seriously the actions and insistent demands of the Japanese, which had been regarded as attempts at intimidation rather than as concrete intentions. The United States, Great Britain and the Netherlands kept only relatively weak garrisons in Asia, and their military equipment was out of date, often having been relegated from the European theatre of war. The troops concerned were accordingly easy to mop up.

The Japanese forces invaded numerous areas which were often vast distances apart. This made it fairly easy to overthrow the Allied defences, and within 5 months the Nipponese tentacles had extended over thousands of kilometres in the realisation of the war-lords' prodigious scheme for the 'Greater East Asian Co-prosperity Sphere', a sort of politico-economic empire which would subjugate populations and exploit the riches of the countries conquered.

In two separate and successive stages[1] Japan had occupied vast spaces and uncontested supremacy not only over Eastern Asia, but also over a large part of the Pacific Ocean. This gigantic offensive made her forces masters of an 'empire' ranging from the Indo-Burmese border in the west to the Gilbert and Ellice Islands in the north to the Indian Archipelago in the south. This represented a circular domain some 9,000 kilometres in diameter. The Allied powers had had successively to abandon the Philippines, Burma, Malaya, Borneo, the Island of Celebes, Sumatra, Java, Timor, Bali, the Aleutian Islands, Guam, Wake, the Gilbert and Ellice Islands, New Britain, New Ireland and the southern coast of New Guinea.

Never had military expansion been so vast or so rapid. Not only had the invasion been accomplished over an extremely brief period, but the Japanese losses had been astonishingly small. Even the most optimistic Japanese expectations had been justified, and the largest Japanese vessel sunk was a destroyer. As for merchant shipping, the losses sustained did not even reach one-twentieth of the overall tonnage available. Casualty figures were also low and very far from reaching the least pessimistic predictions. Neither Japan's naval air arm nor her military air-reconnaissance squadrons suffered the destruction of more than a few hundred aircraft for a list of victories and tactical successes of outstanding brilliance. Japan's achievement was complete from the strategical, territorial and tactical points of view.

The psychological climate in Japan

Whereas in the Allied camp, and especially in the United States, the first five months of war had produced anxiety and discouragement, the state of mind in Japan was one of intense euphoria. Not

[1] Cf. the author's 'La Guerre du Pacifique ' Vol. I, 'The Japanese Expansion', published by Editions Robert Laffont, Paris 1968.

only were the victories real and tangible; propaganda exalted and magnified them, paying tribute to the already rich and ineffable glory of this, the Japanese military milennium. The dizziest dreams of ascendancy were born, developed and took shape.

The Japanese people had been consciously conditioned by propaganda and were ready to accept the greatest sacrifices, knowing that victory would only be obtained at great expense. The people could now see however that their leaders had not lied and that the imperial forces of Japan were indomitable. They saw that nothing had been able to stop the advance of their soldiers and that defences had crumbled before the power and determination of their warriors. But there was more. Already conditioned by the news of so many victories, they discovered that the ancient myth of white supremacy and the invincibility of the white races had dissolved and, in so doing, had given a new dimension to the war. They realised that they had just thrown off the shackles of this inferiority complex and were now and henceforth an adult, sovereign and paramount people.

The Empire of the Rising Sun had already vanquished the Russians in 1905, but that victory had been tempered with the knowledge that the Czarist régime was already toppling and the Russian revolution impending. This time, however, their enthusiasm was boundless and unreserved. The foes who were now biting the dust consisted of an alliance of three great European nations, proud warriors of the white races who had surrendered to or been put to flight by the indomitable soldiers of the Mikado. Enemy generals were giving themselves up, cities were falling and the flag of Nippon was flying above vast areas over which a few months before they would not have dared to claim supremacy. Such brilliant victories, which were as swift as they were cheap in terms of lives and losses, triggered off an unprecedented patriotic fervour, and even the least enthusiastic Japanese could not but share in the general euphoria.

Paradoxically, such lyrical transports, which were all the stronger in a people steeped in military traditions, flowed upstream as it were, until they reached the ruling military hierarchy. Generals and officers alike realised from the current mood of patriotic exaltation that they could rely unreservedly on the future support of an ardent people. The result was that a kind of megalomania took hold of Japan. Nothing was impossible, and everything appeared to be more or less attainable. Nevertheless, the objectives during the first and second phases of Japan's military expansion had been regarded as the extreme limit of her claims and also the extreme limit of her capacity. Certain noble dignitaries had even doubted the success of some of these claims, but now these claims had all been made good and, what is more, at a disconcertingly high speed and a surprisingly low cost.

Henceforth this feeling of power and invincibility and the exceptional prestige accorded Japan's armed forces as a result of their victories combined to re-awaken her dreams of ambitious and limitless conquest. The pride of the Japanese populace in their armed forces was now accompanied by a burning faith in the justice of the war they had undertaken. From the proletariat to the summit of the hierarchy, the Japanese nourished national ambitions of splendour and infinite conquest and dreamed of universal domination. Never had the secular philosophy of Hakko Ichiu been so near fulfilment or so vividly illustrated.

The above may not seem rational, but why should the Japanese not have been filled with enthusiasm for these successes which would have been undreamed of a few years earlier? Why should they not believe in the reality of the victories and the formidable military might wielded by their country? Why not give way to their violent desire for ethnic and economic expansion? Why not turn the tables by shaking loose the psychological fetters imposed on them by the whites who had exploited the coveted riches of Asia? Why should this poor but imaginative people, brought up in a tradition of martial glory and religious exaltation, not feel justified in believing that their hour of glory had come and that the gods were leading them towards a solemn and dedicated destiny?

All the arguments were in favour of national pride which was also racial in origin and which would henceforth know no bounds. Did not the spectacular conquests represent the realisation of Hakko Ichiu's theory that Japan would, in this milennium, be called upon to dominate the world?

The strategic choices

Given such popular acclaim of the sensational victories achieved in the initial stages of Japanese expansion, it was predictable and even desirable that the expansion so far undertaken should be extended. Obviously, military circles were thinking along these lines and seeking to exploit their victories by taking advantage of the almost untouched potential of the Japanese forces. The result was that new plans were made for conquests that were as ambitious as the inflamed minds of the Japanese at that time. Their territorial claims were such that the plans to make them effective would have been regarded as insane only a few months before, but nobody even smiled at such ideas now. There was no reason to doubt their efficacy, since all the moral and physical barriers concerned, even those reputed to be unshakable in their taboo, such as the presence of the whites in Asia, had crumbled under Japanese pressure.

Nevertheless, a military controversy arose on the matter as a direct result of the permanent state of rivalry between the Japanese Army and Navy. In all periods of history there have been many countries whose two basic services were opposed to each other's interests and prestige, but in Japan the Army and Navy were two separate and powerful entities, each of which represented a state within the state. Their disagreement on matters of principle was sometimes so violent as to produce an absolute refusal to co-operate, a complete inability to understand each other's problems, and often contempt for the national interest. Now, when it was essential to discuss plans to exploit the victorious offensive of the first few months of the war, Army and Navy were sharply and profoundly divided on the question of aims.

Paradoxically enough, the opinions expressed only a few months before, now, in the early spring of 1942, underwent a complete reversal. The Army, which had been the main instigator of and decisive factor in the great military expansion, now maintained that the conflict should be static in order to consolidate, reinforce and systematically exploit the riches of the conquered territories. As far as the Army was concerned, their aim had been achieved and they advised taking their profit now by rendering impregnable the areas they had invaded.

In this, the Japanese Generals had abandoned two grandiose projects which their German allies had suggested. These were (a) to invade the Soviet Union from the south-east and thus clamp Stalin's armies in a vice, and (b) to overrun India, continue the offensive towards the west, seize the oil-bearing regions in the Middle East and join up with Rommel's Afrikakorps. These two enticing plans had been carefully studied, but were rejected in the end because of the enormous effective forces and extensive logistics required, problems which were well-nigh insoluble in relation to invasions at such vast distances from home.

The Admirals of the Imperial Japanese Navy, on the other hand, who had approved the initial military expansion only with great reluctance and with a bad grace, now advocated extending the conquests achieved as a vital and essential necessity.

The above about-face on the part of the services may appear inexplicable and even baffling, but they were based on proven facts. We know that the Imperial Fleet had taken a very active part in the military expansion and had sustained negligible losses, so that this arm of the Japanese forces was virtually intact at the end of these initial victories.

From one point of view, it was desirable that the Fleet should not remain inactive and be employed solely as a watch-dog, but it was becoming increasingly necessary to extend the perimeter of the area already occupied by putting around it a girdle of operational bases which would act as a shield against attacks from outside the territories already subjected. On the other hand, there was no doubt that the Western Powers would, sooner or later, emerge from their present tactical situation and that the Navy ought to be provided with bases which would enable the war at sea to be pursued well away from the conquered lands and preserve the spoils gained from them.

Admiral Isoroku Yamamoto, Chief of the Combined Fleet, had said prior to hostilities that he could guarantee a series of uninterrupted victories for a period of between six and twelve months, but that he could not accept responsibility for what happened afterwards. This was true. Like a number of other officers in the Japanese Navy, Yamamoto was well acquainted with the United States and their redoubtable industrial potential. He knew that only another extensive blow would prevent the Allies from recovering from their wounds and slowly, but inexorably eroding the initial Japanese victories.

The Navy therefore put forward several plans for extending the military offensive, all of which were designed to destroy the United States Navy and take over the bases from which the distant but inevitable Allied counter-offensive would be launched. The Naval Staff were anxious regarding the future and at the back of their minds was the thought that at Pearl Harbor it was only battleships which had been destroyed or put out of action for a lengthy period. The aircraft carriers of the United States Pacific fleet had been spared and now represented a disquieting threat to the conquests made by Japan.

These arguments, which were of course logical and irrefutable, nevertheless masked a psychotic state of mind which needs to be examined. The fact was that the Naval Staff knew better than anyone the status of the United States in the Allied camp and they were probably the only ones, in the atmosphere of general euphoria, to make a correct evaluation of the Japanese successes. They realised that Japan had just carried off an incredible victory, like a mouse triumphing over a cat. They were, it is true, aware of their power, but they were not so stupid as to think it would last; the difference in the industrial levels of the two countries was too great for that. They therefore needed to pull off a new and resounding master-stroke which would keep their adversary paralysed and at the same time prolong their impunity.

There was one other possibility, old, it is true, but rejuvenated by the rush of delirious fervour resulting from the initial victories. This was an enterprise both grandiose and impractical, but nonetheless dear to the hearts of the Japanese Naval Staff, namely the invasion of Australia, or at the very least her northern provinces. The Australian continent had always had a sort of fascination for the Japanese who saw in its vast territories a possible realisation of their dreams of expanding both ethnically and hegemonically. Behind their traditional mysticism, lay the Navy's awareness that Australia would probably serve as a spring-board from which the Allies could ultimately launch their inevitable counter-offensive. For these reasons, conquest of the continent of Australia would on the one hand provide an objective for Japan's as yet still imaginary apotheosis and at the same time put off, perhaps for ever, any counter-offensive on the part of her enemies.

Although the Naval Staff had doubtless felt elated by the initial military successes, they were at the same time aware of the strategic realities of the situation. The Navy's general plan envisaged therefore the invasion of the northern part of Australia (roughly the north-eastern third) the conquest of New Caledonia, the Fiji Islands and Samoa. This project, which they vehemently advocated, would give them absolute mastery of the Coral Sea and, simultaneously, of the entire south-eastern part of the area on the perimeter of the lands they already held. In addition, the Japanese forces would be able to bar the Allies from using the vital route between the United States and Australia, without which it would be impossible for them to regain any of their lost territories.

This was a very attractive plan, but it did not appeal to the Army who saw in it an expansion, an expenditure of energy and, above all, an undue extension of their lines of communication, which they wanted to avoid at all costs. The divergence of opinion took on alarming proportions and split the military leaders into two camps. It was several weeks before any step forward emerged from their discussions or, what is worse, before any measures were taken to apply the principles involved. The result was that, when the time came for action, plans had to be improvised or at least hastily put into action. Rather curiously, it was the Americans who quite unconsciously tipped the scale in favour of the Japanese Navy.

When the Navy's idea, in face of fierce military opposition, was finally adopted however, the Navy was obliged to limit its objectives in order to obtain the Army's support which was both reluctantly and grudgingly given. This plan had long been germinating in the mind of Admiral Yamamoto, indeed ever since the results of the surprise attack on Pearl Harbor were announced. It entailed the destruction of the enemy's aircraft carriers, those venomous American spear-heads, and the extension of Japanese conquests to the south-west Pacific as an insurance against the future.

In the meantime, however, what had the Americans been doing to provoke this opinion of their aircraft carriers and, what is more important, to cause the Japanese to crystallise their arguments into this one final decision?

The threat to Australia

During the second stage of their military breakthrough, the Japanese had landed on the north coast of New Guinea and had immediately set up air bases along its length. Now, since the beginning of March 1942, Japanese naval aircraft had been taking off from Lae and Salamaua, and, somewhat later, from Buna, crossing the Owen Stanley Mountains and wreaking destruction on Port Moresby on the southern coast of New Guinea, where there was an Allied air base. A considerable amount of air fighting developed and tons of explosives were dropped, but, against all expectation, the Japanese forces did not manage to wipe the name of Port Moresby from the map. The Japanese had banked on their success which would have left Australia, which was very close,[1] open to their attacks. Despairing

[1] Cape York, which marks the northernmost tip of Australia, is separated from the southern coast of New Guinea by the Torres Straits which are only 160 kilometres (100 miles) across.

of achieving their goal by air, the Japanese were later to open a vain and senseless onslaught by land across an exceptionally unwelcoming terrain.

But, although Japan's sights were already fixed on Australia, in Tokyo there was as yet no thought of invading her. The idea was simply to present the continent with a direct and paralysing threat. It was, incidentally, at this point that discussions began between the Army and the Navy on the possibility of prolonging their original offensive. Tokyo was playing on Australian nerves, and, on March 11, 1942, the Japanese Prime Minister, Hideki Tojo, delivered his first solemn warning:

> 'Australia must learn that defence against our invincible forces is impossible in view of her sparse population, the vastness of her territories and her geographical position which makes her so distant from both the United States and Britain.'

On the following day, March 12, at a special meeting of the Japanese Parliament, Tojo became more specific and also more threatening:

> 'Australia and New Zealand are now threatened directly by the might of the Imperial forces, and both of them should know that any resistance is futile. If the Australian government does not modify her present attitude, their continent will suffer the same fate as the Dutch East Indies.'

The latter had, of course, just fallen to Japanese forces, whose offensive was victorious on all fronts, and Canberra was living under the fear of imminent invasion, Tojo was right! The United States and Great Britain were very far away and appeared to be incapable of intervening, but on March 13, John Curtin, the Australian Prime Minister, made his famous appeal:

> 'This is a warning. Australia is the last Allied bastion between the west coast of America and Japan. If she succumbs, the entire American Continent will be wide open to invasion. Some people think that the Japanese will by-pass Australia and that they will be intercepted and destroyed in the Indies. But, I tell you that saving Australia will be the same as saving the western side of the United States. However that may be, Australia will, if invaded, fight to the last man and will apply the scorched earth policy.'

John Curtin was hardly dramatising the situation. Australia was not only threatened but cut off from her allies. Great Britain had been brutally expelled from her Asian colonies and was at grips with Hitler's Germany. As for the United States, she had lost her battleships at Pearl Harbor and her four aircraft carriers could not be everywhere at once; the Pacific was much too vast.

The first American reactions

John Curtin's appeal was unneeded. Some ten weeks earlier, on January 1, 1942, the American Chiefs of Staff had decided what line to take. America knew that Australia was indispensable and that, whatever the cost, it was essential to hold on to a long concave line between the Aleutian Islands and Australia, passing through Midway, the Phoenix, Samoan and Fijian Islands and New Caledonia. Already large numbers of vessels were supplying Australia with men and munitions in unbroken succession. The United States knew, too, that she could undertake nothing on a large scale as long as her war machine was not operating at full power.

Nevertheless, a number of secondary actions had taken place. These were intended to train officers and men for subsequent operations and also to 'take stock of' the Japanese defences. On February 1, for instance, a Task Group[1] centred on the aircraft carrier *Yorktown* and commanded by Rear-Admiral Fletcher had attacked the island of Makin in the Gilbert and Ellice Islands and the islands of Jaluit and Mili in the southern part of the Marshall Islands. Another group centred on the aircraft carrier *Enterprise* under the command of Vice-Admiral William F. Halsey, raided the islands of Wotje, Maloelap and Kwajalein which also formed part of the Marshall Islands. These two raids had not done much damage to Japanese installations, but they sowed the seeds of anxiety and constrained the Japanese High Command to allocate defence forces to the Central Pacific which would have been very useful elsewhere.

Meanwhile, the situation in the south-west Pacific was disturbing the Allies. They knew that the Japanese were concentrating troops at Rabaul (New Britain) and at Kavieng (New Ireland). They also knew that an enemy offensive towards the south was a possibility. The Allies feared that Japanese forces would attack New Caledonia and the New Hebrides. The Japanese, intoxicated by their victories,

[1] Also known as Task Forces, groups of this type consisted of a varying number of ships brought together to carry out a set mission. This was a very flexible method developed by the Americans from experience gained in raids.

could thus at any moment have taken advantage of the initiative they had gained and start operations.

For this reason, any American reaction, however limited, would have been welcome, even if it were only to discourage enemy claims in this sector. Then, in mid-February, the United States Navy assigned the Task Group from the aircraft carrier *Lexington* under the command of Vice-Admiral Wilson Brown to the senior command of Vice-Admiral Herbert F. Leary who had been seconded to Australia.

An air attack on the enemy base at Rabaul was mounted, but on February 20, within a short distance from their objective, the American Task Group was spotted and attacked by two waves of Japanese twin-engined bombers. The situation was grave from a tactical point of view; the American fighter pilots on board had had little experience, and the huge aircraft carrier found herself dangerously exposed to the enemy. The anti-aircraft defences of the *Lexington* were neither very effective nor accurate, but she was saved by the action of an extremely brave pilot, Lieutenant O'Hare. In his single-seat Grumman F4F Wildcat fighter, O'Hare courageously flew at the most threatening of the enemy squadrons and brought down five bombers in four minutes, forcing the others to release their bombs at random, while the other fighter pilots chased off the rest of the bombers. Admiral Wilson Brown, who no longer had the advantage of surprise and who realised that his valuable vessel was vulnerable, wisely decided to withdraw.

American Naval GHQ were following the operation hour by hour and decided to carry out more raids of this type in order to distract Japanese attention to other sectors and so split up their forces. On February 24, the *Enterprise* Task Group under Vice-Admiral Halsey, attacked Wake Island, which had recently been taken by the Japanese, and then, at dawn on March 4, proceeded to strike at Marcus Island, less than 1,000 miles from Tokyo.

Here, too, no one could say that the damage inflicted on the enemy was irreparable, but the diversion which had been the aim of the previous raids appeared to be working. The Americans had the impression that the Japanese were, to some small extent, loosening their hold on the south-west Pacific in order to send troops to the defence of their threatened positions in the central Pacific. This feeling was of course no more than an impression, since the Japanese forces were still very active in the south-western part of the ocean and the threat they posed in this sector was such that Admiral Leary decided to carry out a new raid, using naval aircraft against the enemy's base at Rabaul.

This time the Task Group was increased to Task Force size and consisted of both the carriers *Yorktown* and *Lexington* together with their escorts of cruisers and destroyers. Vice-Admiral Wilson Brown also set out, but, on March 8, when the Japanese landings at Lae and Salamaua on the north coast of New Guinea were announced, the operation was diverted so as to ward off these more pressing dangers. And, of course, a raid against these very recently established bridge-heads could have disastrous effects on the enemy.

Wilson Brown hesitated. Would it be better to make a frontal attack on the Japanese amphibious forces on the north coast or to surprise them by aircraft alone, attacking from the south coast? This second alternative was made possible by the width of New Guinea at this spot, even though it entailed flying over the high mountains of the Owen Stanley range. The Admiral decided in favour of caution and penetrated the Gulf of Papua, leaving part of his escort in the vicinity of the Louisiade Archipelago in order to cover himself against any naval attack by the enemy.

On March 10, the American carrier's 103 aircraft took off and headed north-west. They crossed the inimical mountain territory by a pass, flying at 8,500 feet and literally swept down on the Japanese who were not expecting an attack from inland. The bridgeheads were badly knocked about and several vessels of the Japanese invasion forces were sunk or damaged. The raid was so successful that the threat to Australia seemed to have been averted, or at least so the Allies thought.

At this juncture, General Douglas MacArthur, Commander-in-Chief of the combined American and Philippine forces, succeeded in fleeing from Corregidor, reaching Australia on March 17 after one of the most hectic circumnavigations ever made. His B.17 aircraft landed at Batchelor Field near Darwin during a Japanese air-raid. Appointed Commander-in-Chief of the Allied forces in the Pacific, MacArthur set up his HQ at Brisbane and put Herbert F. Leary in command of the sparse naval forces available in this sector. MacArthur did not take up his new duties until April 18.

We have spent some time on the American raids, which were in themselves minor ones of secondary importance, because of their originality on the one hand and their ultimate consequences on the other. In their immediate context, they were, as we have seen, mere pinpricks, but they enabled the American forces involved to get used to the war and acquire an invaluable measure of operational training. They also revived the confidence of the American civilian population in general and servicemen in particular, in all of whom morale had been on the verge of disintegrating. The raids occurred at a moment when bad news was coming in from all sides. Whether from Malaya, Burma, the Indian Archipelago, the Philippines or elsewhere, the news was one of defeat, relinquishment or surrender.

Lastly, the revival of the Allies' fighting spirit represented by these raids had the effect of to some extent dispersing the Japanese forces who were obliged to defend very widely scattered positions, but, what was beyond doubt of the greatest importance, was the presence of the aircraft carriers which had survived Pearl Harbor. The mere fact of their existence and the proof they had given of their effectiveness along very different sectors of the vast Pacific Ocean made them the only really positive elements opposing the Japanese High Command.

On the basis of these facts, Admiral Yamamoto became convinced that nothing could be attempted in the way of fresh military expansion as long as the menace of American naval aircraft was hovering overhead. As far as the Admiral was concerned, it was essential to destroy as soon as possible the last really effective weapon in the hands of the enemy, namely their aircraft carriers. If these could be effectively overpowered, it would be a long time before they recovered. It is true that Admiral Yamamoto, like many other members of the Japanese High Command, was entranced by the prospect of extending Japanese sovereignty to Australia and the South Seas, but he postulated that the American naval forces' air power, which was the only serious obstacle in the way of this achievement, should first be destroyed.

Now, obviously, the destruction of the American aircraft carriers would have given the Japanese complete freedom of movement for their troops, safety for their supply lines and a chance for the Army to consolidate its victories before their adversaries could re-muster a force which was capable of seriously threatening the 'Greater East Asian Co-prosperity Sphere'.

Japanese plans

Despite the logic of his plan, Admiral Yamamoto did not receive the support he expected, even less the permission to put it into effect. Japanese official circles retorted that any such project was merely hypothetical and would require too many vessels.

What then, precisely, had Yamamoto proposed?

The Admiral had suggested challenging the enemy in his own waters, forcing him to give battle and destroying him by sheer numerical superiority. This would of course involve a great part of the Imperial fleet but the fleet ought to be able to exhibit the required superiority at any time and in any place, and this would guarantee success. In order to make sure that the Americans would not refuse to fight, Yamamoto wished to proceed to the Hawaiian Islands, which was the traditional haunt of the U.S. fleet in the Pacific, land on Midway and from there threaten to attack the base at Pearl Harbor. This threat would be too direct for the Americans not to react.

Apart from a battle in which the Japanese could not but inflict crushing defeat on their enemies, Yamamoto saw no obstacle to extending Japanese military domination to Australia. In this he was supported by a fairly large number of naval officers, but he had to contend not only with other strategical points of view within Imperial Naval HQ itself, but also with conditions imposed by the Army. In this context, the Imperial Army was fiercely opposed to landing in Australia, because the generals felt unable to recruit, equip and feed the twelve divisions required for a force of this nature. Their refusal was arbitrary and final.

At this stage, another point of view was expressed among the Naval Staff. This view, which gradually gained credence and resulted in the compromise which offended fewest, viz. the 'Australian doctrine', was first thought out and enunciated by Captain Sadatoshi Tomioka, Head of the Project Section at Naval HQ. This doctrine was based on the principle that Australia constituted or would later constitute the ideal spring-board for a future Allied counter-offensive and that, for this reason, it was essential not to lose sight of the strategic importance of the Australian continent. Since the Army had refused its support for this theory, there was no longer any point in invading the northern provinces, but it was important to block any possible attempt to reinforce the Allied forces who were already based in Australia. The aim was to isolate the great Dominion and perhaps to make her resign from the conflict by signing a separate peace treaty.

The proposed blockade could be applied tactically by occupying Port Moresby on the south coast of New Guinea and strategically by invading New Caledonia and the archipelagos of Fiji and Samoa. The route between the United States and Australia would thus be permanently cut off.

This plan depended on considerable participation by the Imperial Navy and thus postponed the large-scale operation postulated by Admiral Yamamoto. To the amazement of those who favoured the 'Australian doctrine', the Army went back on its decision and agreed to take part in the project now that its objectives had been reduced.

Nevertheless, the dispute had not yet been settled. Yamamoto's supporters were still vehemently upholding the cardinal significance of their project on the principle that it would be madness to design and execute an amphibious operation before destroying the American aircraft carriers. Their opponents retorted that it was essential to exploit the advantages reaped from their past conquests while the Allies were still out of breath, and to act before they were reinforced, particularly since the destruction of the American carriers was still only hypothetical and not at all certain.

On April 2, 1942, a new discussion broke out between the adherents of the two schemes, but their arguments led to no formal policy. The spokesmen of both parties set out their principles, but numerous points remained unresolved. In the event, there was a certain swing in favour of the 'Australian' school of thought, at first because it tended to unite the extreme points of view and, later, because it had already started to be put into action.

Against this background, the occupation of Bougainville and the north coast of New Guinea together with the aerial war being waged on Port Moresby were so many aiming-points on the way to realising the objectives pursued by those in favour of the 'Australian doctrine'. For these reasons, too, there was a tendency to agree with it in mid-April, but this agreement had only been reached because naval requirements for the operation were moderate and did not entail the use of the great number of vessels, which Admiral Yamamoto's scheme required.

The Japanese were underestimating the power of their adversaries, and they showed a disturbing tendency to despise them once they had breathed the heady perfume of their recent easy victories. Their most serious calculations assessed the number of aircraft based in

Australia at 200 plus one aircraft carrier likely to find her way to the Coral Sea, namely the *Saratoga*.

Japan's final plans

However paradoxical it may appear, it was the Americans who decided events and who forced the Japanese to crystallise their plans. On April 18, 1942, there occurred the Doolittle raid[1] which marked a decisive triumph for the school of Yamamoto and his supporters. The threat from the east, ie. from the Pacific Ocean, was only too real and the paramount feeling was that the American aircraft carriers should be destroyed before they had a chance to make any further strikes of this kind.

Not only had Yamamoto obtained full agreement to his proposals; he even managed to fix the date for his operations as the first week in June. This complete overthrow of his original plans was to have highly significant consequences in the pursuit of other objectives. When Colonel Takushiro Hattori, Head of Army Strategy and Operations, was informed of these arrangements, he readily concurred. The Midway affair involved the Army to only a very limited extent, and furthermore, since the Australian invasion would not now take place, the Army would not have to reduce its deployment on the China or Manchuria front.

Complete approval was thus reached in the last week in June, and the following shows the final analysis of the operations to be undertaken:

(1) Occupy Tulagi in the southern Solomon Islands so as to have a naval air base to control the northern part of the Coral Sea. Follow this up with a landing at Port Moresby in the south-east part of New Guinea so as to bring Northern Australia within range of Japanese aircraft. This stage was known as Operation *MO*.[2]

(2) Carry out the great attack on Midway and occupy strong points in the Aleutian Islands to trigger off a decisive naval battle.

(3) Once these two operations were complete, the Japanese were to overrun the Fiji and Samoa Archipelagos so as to cut off once and for all the life-line between the United States and Australia.

[1] This was a reprisal raid carried out by the Americans with 16 twin-engined North American B.25 Mitchell Army bombers embarked in the aircraft carrier *Hornet*. This raid caused only a very small amount of damage, but it produced a great deal of disquiet in Japan.

[2] *MO*: The first two letters of the Japanese name for Port Moresby.

It is clear from this general plan that the 'Australian' school of thought had won its case by giving priority to Operation *MO*. It was because the supporters of the 'Australian doctrine' had so vehemently insisted on the need to profit from the enemy's unfavourable situation and to strike while the iron was hot, that Operation *MO* had been put first on the list. This priority was, however, also due to the fact that the initial phases had already begun.

The die was thus cast, and the storm would soon be rumbling over the Coral Sea. This vast area of ocean was given its name by the British naval captain Matthew Flinders, who in 1803 had first explored it and had been delighted with its mild climate, the gentle freshness of its south-east trade winds, its almost unvarying temperature in both summer and winter, its superb coral reefs and the impressive luxuriance of the islands it lapped against. He also noted that its translucent waters were seldom disturbed by typhoons or tempests.

A few days later, the General Staff spokesman at the HQ of the Imperial Navy summarised Japanese intentions in the following words:

> 'We shall first occupy Port Moresby, together with important positions at Tulagi and in south-east New Guinea, by close collaboration between the Navy and a detachment of South-Sea forces. We shall set up air bases and intensify our air operations on the Australian sector. Later, one of our groups will occupy the islands of Nauru and Ocean so as to ensure a supply of the phosphates so much needed by our agriculture.'

From the point of view of the higher-ranking Japanese officers who were in the know, this general plan was attractive, and none of them was in any doubt as to its victorious outcome. Dazzled by earlier successes and therefore accustomed to triumphing over these contemptible 'soldiers with fish eyes',[1] the Japanese regarded these new objectives as an extension of their initial military offensive, which, like the latter, could only result in complete and decisive victory.

Although during the first and second stages of the Japanese military expansion, certain victories had been predicted as easy or as likely to be relatively unresisted by the enemy, these victories had involved fighting. It was now known that there would be battles, but the

[1] Contemptuous term used by the Japanese to describe all white combatants in general and the Allies in particular.

enemy's forces were considered to be so poor and the individual combatants so demoralised that the result was beyond doubt.

Whether this applied to the Midway engagement, when the bulk of the Imperial fleet would be afloat, or to Port Moresby where the ratio of the forces was obviously still in Japan's favour, the Japanese Chiefs of Staff had unlimited confidence in their weapons and were completely certain of winning. This view of theirs was due to slight errors in their estimates of the forces confronting them, and also to their recently acquired and deceptive feeling of superiority. For these reasons, too, the number of ships available for Operation *MO* had been calculated as a minimum, but was considered to be adequate and in any case superior to the resources assumed to be available to the enemy.

Operation *MO*

In view of the fact that the bulk of the Imperial fleet was to be used in the Midway and Aleutian Islands engagements, there was no question of using the same vessels for Operation *MO*. This was because they would have insufficient time to rearm at base before setting off on the great Midway venture. In simple terms, the Imperial Naval HQ were hoping that the two aircraft carriers assigned to operations in the south would join up at sea with the Midway forces. The fact that their naval resources could be divided in this way is a fair indication of the naval potential possessed by the Japanese at that time.

The detailed plans for Operation *MO* can be set out as follows:

(1) One landing group, consisting of the 22nd Destroyer Division, one troopship, one seaplane transport, one minelayer and several lighter vessels, to seize the island of Tulagi and its valuable anchorage;

(2) One group centred on one seaplane transport and consisting of two light cruisers, three gunboats and one mine-layer, to proceed to the Louisiade Archipelago and establish an air base;

(3) One landing group proper, consisting of eleven troopships carrying both military and naval personnel, one light cruiser accompanying the 6th Destroyer Flotilla and various supply vessels, to seize the airstrips in the area round Port Moresby;

(4) One so-called covering group, comprising one light aircraft carrier, four battle-cruisers, one destroyer and one fuel tanker, to

guard the logistic approaches by air and sea during the landing operation at Port Moresby;

(5) One so-called striking force, made up of two large tactical aircraft carriers, two battle-cruisers, six destroyers and one fuel tanker, to intervene from a distance should the enemy put in an appearance by sea;

(6) One look-out group, consisting of seven submarines, to patrol over a wide radius so as to give warning of any action taken by the enemy;

(7) Lastly, the 25th air group, which was responsible for shore-based naval aircraft, to support the various naval squadrons by both long- and short-range reconnaissances and bombing attacks.

As always, when the Japanese were dealing with relatively large forces, their command and operational structure was extremely complex and was reflected in a series of intricate sub-commands based on the rank of each squadron commander in the hierarchy and his personal authority within his division.

The Tulagi group was under the command of Rear-Admiral Kiyohide Shima, while the group attacking the Louisiade Archipelago was assigned to Rear-Admiral Marushige. The Port Moresby group was commanded by Rear-Admiral Sadamichi Kajioka, the covering group by Rear-Admiral Aritomo Goto, the shock force by Vice-Admiral Takeo Takagi, the look-out group by Captain Ishizaki and the shore-based aircraft by Rear-Admiral Sadayoshi Yamada. All these commands were subordinated to the higher authority of Vice-Admiral Shigeyoshi Inoue, Commander-in-Chief of the 4th Imperial fleet, which was known as the South-Sea fleet because it was from the South Seas that most of the vessels taking part in Operation *MO* had come.[1]

The operation was divided into separate and distinct actions in its initial stages, so that each tactical group should follow a particular route and time-table in accomplishing its mission. Then, in the second stage, the various groups were to repair to the vicinity of Port Moresby in order to lend a hand in the landing itself. To this end, the Japanese plan recommended all groups to use the Jomard Passage in the area round the islands of Deboyne and Misima. This

[1] See Appendix 1 for Table of Organisation and Composition of the Japanese Naval Air Arm.

would minimise their sailing time and they would be able to pass unperceived through these large numbers of islets. The ships thus assembled would then constitute a western force which would be under the command of Admiral Goto.

The striking force, on the other hand, on the eastern flank, was to come down from Truk, pass outside the Solomon Islands heading south-east, then turn due west and head for Port Moresby. This force was to enter the Coral Sea the instant there was any sign of enemy activity. If there were, the enemy would be caught between two fires, Goto's in the west and Takagi's, who would be arriving from the east, respectively. As the Japanese had assessed the American naval potential in this area at only one aircraft carrier, optimism was the order of the day, and the Japanese sailors had the greatest possible faith in the outcome.

Bearing in mind that the aim of Operation *MO* was to turn the Allied base at Port Moresby into a Japanese fortress and to gain control of the Coral Sea, it is clear that this policy, if it were successful, would inevitably cut off Australia from her allies, in particular the United States, and perhaps oblige her to resign from the conflict. Moreover, in order to make the Australians fully aware of the fate looming over them, the Japanese had arranged that immediately after the battle, which would of course be decided in their favour, their carrier-based aircraft would execute a series of destructive raids on North Queensland. The Japanese planes would bomb Thursday Island in the extreme north and the cities of Coen, Cooktown and Townsville, where they counted on wiping out the vessels and aircraft based there. All their arrangements were therefore complete and they were now ready to attack objectives which were strategic and, at the same time, political. The great Japanese military expansion was about to be extended to the South Seas.

The American arrangements

As we know, the initial stage of this operation had begun a long time before, and, when the Japanese air attacks on Port Moresby became more numerous and insistent, which they did from April 10 onwards, American attention was drawn to the strategic importance of this sector. A number of factors, in particular some unusual naval movements, suggested that a large-scale operation was being prepared by the Japanese. There were two possible objects of such an operation: an attack might be made either southwards on Port

Moresby or New Caledonia or, northwards on the Ellice Islands or the New Hebrides in the South Pacific.

American reckoning favoured the first of these possibilities, since it was obvious that Port Moresby would offer the enemy a tempting and immediately exploitable target. Also, on April 17 Admiral Chester W. Nimitz, Commander-in-Chief of the Pacific Fleet (CINCPAC) received from his decoding section two very significant items of information. We now know that the United States had obtained the key to the 'Purple' code, the code used for secret messages by the Imperial Navy, and enemy telegrams had been intercepted. This had enabled American experts to decipher Japanese radio communications.

American Intelligence was therefore able to report that (a) an enemy landing force, containing troopships and the light carrier *Shoho*, had set off from Rabaul and would reach its objective on May 3 while (b) two large aircraft carriers would be leaving Truk (in the Caroline Islands) for the Coral Sea. Although the name of their objective had been indecipherable, Admiral Nimitz was certain that this could only be Port Moresby. In this he shared the opinion of General MacArthur, who regarded Port Moresby as the key to the entire Allied defence system and the base from which they would launch their eventual counter-offensive.

The Pacific Ocean had formerly been divided into several command zones, and the command embracing Australia, New Guinea, the eastern half of the Coral Sea, the Indian Archipelago, Borneo and the Philippines had rightfully fallen within the command of MacArthur in view of his abilities and his first-class knowledge of the area concerned. However, it did not seem logical that a general should direct naval operations, and it was therefore decided that any action at sea should be the responsibility of Admiral Nimitz, an overlapping of authority which was to have deplorable consequences.

Although the Americans were in possession of highly valuable information regarding the enemy's movements, they still had to deploy the few pieces they retained on the board. Of the five American aircraft carriers in the Pacific fleet, the *Saratoga* was licking her wounds in Puget Sound, while the *Enterprise* and the *Hornet* had not yet returned from their mission in the West Pacific where they had carried out Colonel Doolittle's attack with the 16 Mitchell bombers. It was worked out that, even by rushing the *Enterprise* and the *Hornet* back to Pearl Harbor and cutting short their replenishment and refitting, these two vessels would not arrive in time to take part in the battle. Only the *Lexington* and the *Yorktown* were available and, of these, the *Yorktown* was the only one of its type near the future area of operations. No battleship was within call, and it was only with difficulty that a sufficient number of cruisers and destroyers could be mustered to form an escort.

Nevertheless Admiral Halsey's return was brought forward to 25th instead of April 26 as arranged, and the Americans set about hastily preparing the *Lexington*. The two aircraft carriers on which Nimitz was counting were also rather different. The *Yorktown* had been taken into service in 1936 and had a displacement of 20,000 tons; the *Lexington*, on the other hand, which had a displacement of 33,000 tons, dated from 1925. Both vessels had taken part in the American reprisal raids in the Central Pacific and on Papua and, in so doing, had become to some extent accustomed to local fighting conditions.

A number of the *Lexington*'s officers and ratings had been with the carrier since she was fitted out and were well aware of the carriers' possibilities. Her aircraft squadrons still lacked training and tactical efficiency, but they included such famous fighter pilots as John S. Thatch and 'Butch' O'Hare, who, it will be recalled, had covered himself with glory during the abortive raid on Rabaul on February 20. The commander of the *Lexington*, Frederick C. Sherman, known as 'Ted', was held in great affection by his crew, and this engendered in the vessel an atmosphere of remarkable stability and confidence. The crew's devotion to the great carrier, which was also shared by the entire United States Navy, had resulted in their giving her the nickname of 'Lady Lex'. The commander of the group centred round the *Lexington* was Rear-Admiral Aubrey W. Fitch, who had taken over from his colleague, Rear-Admiral Wilson Brown, on April 3.

The other carrier, the *Yorktown*, was at that time based at Noumea in New Caledonia. Under Captain Buckmaster, she took on board Rear-Admiral Frank Jack Fletcher who was responsible for Task Force 17, ie. the group of ships centred on the *Yorktown*. A third naval force was also to take part in the Allies' counter-offensive. This was Task Force 44 commanded by the forceful British Admiral, J. C. Crace.[1] When MacArthur had taken over his command in Australia, Vice-Admiral Herbert F. Leary had become Chief of

[1] See Appendix 2 for Table of Allied Organisation and Composition.

Naval Air Forces in the south-west Pacific, forces known familiarly, but somewhat ironically as 'MacArthur's Fleet'.

The unmistakable threat to Australia had thus caused the American commander to provide maximum support by sending three cruisers and by undertaking to be responsible for aerial reconnaissance over the entire zone under his command. Two of these three cruisers, the *Australia* and the *Hobart*, were Australian, and for this reason Rear-Admiral J. C. Crace of the Royal Navy had been chosen to command the group as a whole. Apart from being a gesture to Admiral Crace's personal bravery, this was a diplomatic act of courtesy to Australia and her grim determination to fight off any invader. Finally, several submarines under Captain Christie were to patrol three strategic areas, viz. the Papuan coast and the Louisiade and Bismarck Archipelagos, in order to detect any hostile approach.

Admiral Nimitz, in his spacious office at Pearl Harbor, was earnestly thinking about the forthcoming confrontation. Although he had great confidence in his subordinates, he could not stifle certain anxieties. It was true that he knew from the Japanese messages intercepted and decoded both the route and the time-table which the enemy would follow. This knowledge was a trump card, but it was still essential to muster sufficient forces to oppose Japanese intentions. He knew that they had three aircraft carriers and a formidable array of escort vessels. He was familiar with the dread efficiency of the Imperial Navy and also with the extraordinary degree to which its naval aircraft pilots were trained. The American Navy's resources in this respect were definitely inferior at this particular moment, and the thought of taking on the enemy with only two aircraft carriers was an alarming one. He could, it was true, rely on Fletcher and the courage of his groups, but would this be enough to withstand the fanatical determination of the Japanese? Admiral Nimitz was a troubled man, and his immediate colleagues could confirm that, about the middle of April, the last of his blond hair turned white.

On April 14, Rear-Admiral Fletcher was ordered to proceed to Tongatabu for replenishment and to prepare for naval air combat. On April 16, the *Lexington* and her escort set off from Pearl Harbor and headed south-west. On April 21, Rear-Admiral Fitch, while still at sea, received instructions to rejoin Fletcher's task group on May 1 at a point known as 'Batchelor's Button', 16°S 161° 45'E, ie. at about 250 miles south-west of the island of Espiritu Santo in the New Hebrides. Task Force 44 under Rear-Admiral Crace was instructed to enter the Coral Sea on May 4, at a point where he would be reinforced by both the heavy-cruiser *Chicago* and the destroyer *Perkins*. He was then to place himself at the disposal of Rear-Admiral Fletcher, who, as the senior ranking officer, would assume command of all Allied naval forces present.

Having taken care of these tactical matters, Admiral Nimitz set to work on his plan of operations, in which he nevertheless included Admiral Halsey's two aircraft carriers, *Hornet* and *Enterprise*. These vessels would arrive at Pearl Harbor on April 25, but they would not be able to put to sea again before 30th at the earliest. Also, Halsey had to cover the 3,500 miles from Pearl Harbor to the Coral Sea and would scarcely be able to arrive before May 15, well after the last date in the Japanese time-table. Nimitz reasoned, however, that the presence of the two carriers would be welcome should the enemy for any reason delay putting his invasion plans into execution. He therefore based his plan on the above premises and sent it to Admiral Ernest J. King, Commander-in-Chief of the United States Navy, who received it at midday on April 29. The orders given were surprisingly simple and laconic:

> 'Rear-Admiral Fletcher will operate in the Coral Sea from May 1 onwards and will be in command of all the forces assigned to him. He will have discretion to take action to intercept the enemy and keep open vital lines of communication between the United States and Australia.'

On the same day, the Australian Government headed by John Curtin was informed of the enemy's intentions and also of the measures taken by the American High Command. As a result, the Australian Cabinet decided on May 1 to evacuate the tiny garrison of Tulagi which had no chance of withstanding the expected onslaught of the Japanese.

Admiral Nimitz's anxiety was due not only to the outcome of the battle which was pending, but also to his need to assess the American reaction to the Japanese threat to the central Pacific. Although American Intelligence knew of the dates and places concerned in the Japanese Navy's preparations and probable strength, they had, on the other hand, no precise data on their objective. The size and number of Japanese vessels, however, suggested that the enemy had designs on American positions which were of prime and highly strategic significance. May 1 was not therefore a day of rest and relaxation for Admiral Nimitz, but a day of extreme tension, for he was holding his cards close to his chest, hoping to stop the Japanese thrust towards the south before regrouping and then launching his forces against the threat looming over the central Pacific.

Nimitz was master of the situation, and the United States Navy Department had been wise to choose him for a post of such vast responsibility despite the fact that he was junior to many of his colleagues.

A native of Texas, Nimitz, who passed out as a naval cadet at the Naval Training School of Annapolis in 1905, was of medium height, and his broad, almost baby-like face hid a great deal of physical vitality and subtlety of mind. A man bold in decision, full of tact and diplomacy and, furthermore, endowed with a great sense of fairness, Admiral Nimitz had been appointed to his present post the day after Pearl Harbor, and although he had been given an apparently herculean task, he had nevertheless performed it with brilliance. He was, in addition, loyally supported by men of high abilities who had no lack of courage.

One of these was Rear-Admiral Frank Jack Fletcher, a man of great height, lean and with a youthful figure. He had just celebrated his fifty-sixth birthday. The lined face, the region surrounding the eyes wrinkled from much staring at the horizon, the firm chin and the wide furrows on each side of the nose, all these reflected a decisive mind and great experience at sea. Although born in Iowa, in the very centre of the United States, Fletcher was a sailor by tradition, a true sea-dog of a type frequently encountered in the era of sailing vessels. The features and, more especially, the fiery eyes showed him to be a man of action accustomed to making quick decisions, but they also gave him a certain attractiveness, even elegance, which caused him to shine at parties and receptions. He played bridge and golf and certainly did not spurn the company of women, with whom he had indisputable success. Proud of both his position and his career, Fletcher used often to say than an officer of the American Navy must first be a sailor, before becoming a fighter.

After distinguishing himself as a young officer in the First World War, Fletcher had knocked about a great deal in the Pacific, and the knowledge of Asia which he had acquired made him a highly able commander. At the moment when the United States were poor in naval resources and forced to fight on several fronts, Fletcher was the most suitable operational leader to head the forces that Nimitz had assembled to repel this new Japanese threat. The course of action and the decisions which Fletcher was to take, and their consequences, never once failed to justify the trust which had been placed in him.

Rabaul, May 1, 1942

The light cruiser *Kashima*, like all the other Japanese vessels moored in the Simpson Roadstead, was gently swinging at anchor. Everything was calm and the ratings were going about their usual business of washing down and painting, whilst others were drowsing in their hammocks. The roadstead, penned in by the peaks surrounding it, seemed to focus the heat of the sun like an oven. From the ships' bridges the town to the north and the four main active volcanoes towering over it could be clearly made out despite a trembling heat haze. A little further away, the roadstead and the White Bay which extended it in the direction of the open sea were hemmed in by other craters. Had it not been for the continuous feeling of insecurity due to the possibility of eruption, this anchorage would have been a haven of peace. Instead, an overwhelming heat prevailed and the air one breathed was hot, humid, sulphurous and impregnated with the fine dust of volcanic ash.

The Navy was privileged; those who had most to complain of in regard to the local climate were the soldiers and air pilots who had to live in this wide-spread desolation consisting of piles of rock, and the fine products of eruptions with almost no fresh water. The outsides of the volcanoes, like the wilderness of the plateaux, had been rapidly converted into an airfield, but the movements of the aircraft raised such clouds of dust that to be a pilot in Rabaul was no sinecure. It required Japanese fanaticism and the imperious needs of war to occupy and subdue this sinister and desolate region.

On board the *Kashima*, converted into a command vessel, Vice-Admiral Shigeyoshi Inoue was in his cabin which also served as an office. This compartment was of modest dimensions and painted white. Through the wide-open port-holes poured blinding light and stifling heat, which a ventilator was trying in vain to reduce. In the middle of the Admiral's office a very ordinary-looking desk was covered with papers. These were reports, service records and plans for Operation *MO*. Lying back in a wooden armchair, the Admiral seemed to be dozing. He was a short man, round, fat and with a chubby face the colour of porcelain. The climate at Rabaul was very lowering, and many Japanese soon took on a pasty and transparent appearance. The Admiral had put on his white tropical uniform but he had not had the courage to button up the neck in temperatures as high as this.

He was thinking, recalling the long story of events which had brought him here, the innumerable reports and telegrams which he had had to send to Tokyo before anybody would take his plans seriously. The Admiral was convinced that he had been the first in the entire navy to suggest this extension of the 'Greater East Asian Co-prosperity Sphere' to the area of the south-west Pacific. He had bombarded the Japanese High Command with requests and proposals to this effect, until he had finally won his case. What was even better, he had been entrusted with the overall command of Operation *MO*. But now the machine was in motion; the first contingent from the fleet, which was intended to overrun Tulagi, had just set off and matters were inexorably taking their course. Every precaution had been taken. It was known that, if the enemy counter-attacked, he would of necessity fall into the trap set for him. The Admiral and all his subordinates were so certain of victory and also so proud of their past successes, so sure of their irresistible might, that it could not be otherwise.

And now that his forces were involved, although reduced as a result of Operation Midway which was being prepared, he felt he had a comfortable margin over the estimated forces of the enemy. The Japanese had been lulled into a state of supreme confidence. Vice-Admiral Inoue knew that this new military expansion could result only in a victory which would yield the keys of Australia to Japan, together with absolute safety over the entire southern sector once the vital line of communication between the United States and Australia was cut. He regarded this plan rather as if it were his own child, and it was with complacent pride that he went through in his mind the successive phases of the operation which had just begun. He stood up and took from the table the thick file containing the plans for Operation *MO*. He examined it for the hundredth time with satisfaction; he went over the details of its execution, but nothing seemed to require refurbishing. He put down the file and reached out for the cup of tea beside him. He drank in little sips, as absent-minded as a romantic poet whose dreams have merged with reality. He saw himself at Port Moresby, issuing new orders, or at Noumea, planning new conquests.

In some forty hours' time he would receive the first reports of

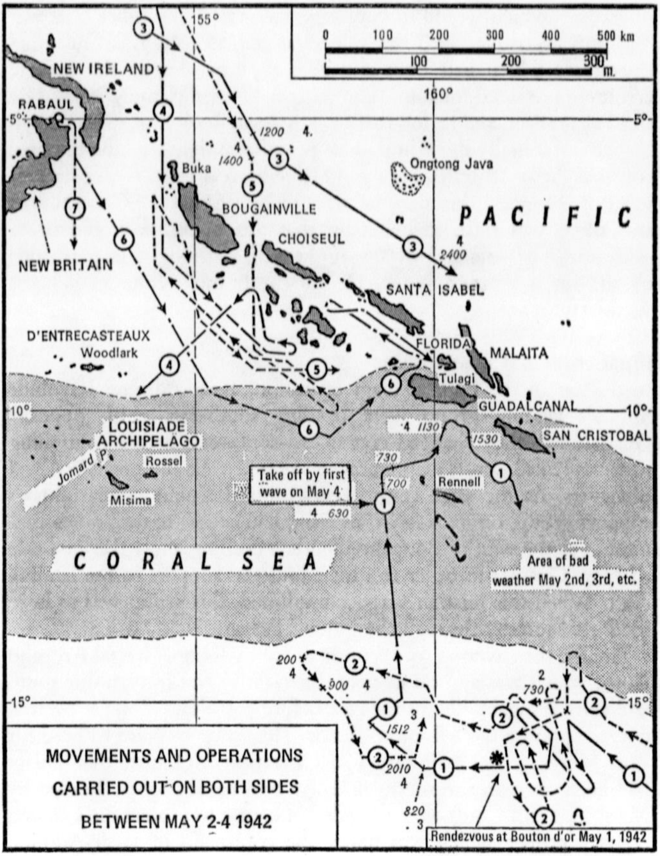

Time notes: eg. 730=0730 hrs (a.m.)

1 Course followed by Task Force 17 under Admiral Fletcher
2 Course followed by ex-Task Force 11 under Admiral Fitch
3 Course followed by Japanese striking force under Admiral Takagi
4 Course followed by Japanese support group under Admiral Marushige
5 Course followed by Admiral Goto's covering group
6 Course followed by Admiral Shima's naval group
7 Course followed by Japanese landing force making for Port Moresby

operations which would of course be victories – any other outcome was inconceivable. Had he not emerged victorious from other operations which had been entrusted to him, despite the meagre resources provided for him? The outcome was absolutely assured by the Takagi fleet, and he felt there was no need to worry, even though he had not initially thought that his proposals might lead the Imperial forces as far as Australia. He would have been satisfied with conquering Port Moresby; but now he was convinced that the General Staff in Tokyo was right in believing that this offensive would bring Australia to her knees. Australia might well, he thought, be persuaded to sue for a separate peace. He caught himself smiling. What a wonderful war!

Japanese naval movements

In pursuit of the initial Tulagi operation, Rear-Admiral Kiyohide Shima's landing group were heading south-east until, opposite Guadalcanal, they changed course east-south-east before continuing towards Florida and Tulagi in order to hoodwink any possible Allied observers. At the same time, Rear-Admiral Kuninori Marushige's support group, on its way from Truk, had orders to turn due south, passing to the west of Bougainville, then cruising along the west side of New Georgia in order to give additional support to the landing craft. When this mission was accomplished, this group was to head for Port Moresby through the Jomard Passage.

Finally, the covering force commanded by Rear-Admiral Aritomo Goto, which was also on its way from Truk, was to turn due south and skirt Bougainville on the east before patrolling along a western course opposite the Solomon Islands. This force was also to head for Port Moresby, the main target of Operation *MO*, now that Tulagi had been overrun and subdued. These two naval groups (headed by Marushige and Goto) were intended of course to protect the invasion convoy proper which was under the command of Rear-Admiral Sadamichi Kajioka, and was as yet still in Rabaul.

Meanwhile, the striking or mobile force, headed by Vice-Admiral Takeo Takagi, which had left Truk on April 29, was still far away in the north between Truk and Bougainville. This was the Japanese naval situation at the moment when Admiral Inoue was smugly studying his files in his cabin on board the *Kashima* at Rabaul.

CHAPTER TWO

Preliminary skirmishes – May, 7 1942

American preparations

As we have seen, Task Force 17 (TF17), commanded by Rear-Admiral Frank J. Fletcher, was waiting in the wings off the New Hebrides. In the clear light of morning on May 1, at about 0615, Task Force 11 (TF11), under the command of Rear-Admiral Aubrey W. Fitch, rejoined the task force centred on the aircraft carrier *Yorktown* 250 miles west of Espiritu Santo. Fletcher took command of the vessels assembled and ordered them to replenish their fuel.

Fletcher started operations by having his own ships (initially TF17) refuelled from the tanker *Neosho* while ordering Fitch to do the same a few miles south-west of him from the tanker *Tippecanoe* at a point where, incidentally, the cruiser *Chicago* and the destroyer *Perkins*, on their way from Noumea, were to rendezvous. Because there were safety precautions to be taken and since there was a delay in the arrival of the *Tippecanoe*, the replenishment operations, particularly in Fitch's case, took a very long time. As a result Fletcher was informed that Fitch would not be able to start refuelling until the evening of May 4. At this moment the covering force, under Admiral Crace, had not yet been formed, and its various units were still on their way to the rendezvous.

Fletcher was annoyed by this contretemps, particularly as he had just received from MacArthur's HQ information concerning the approach of several enemy naval forces. He calculated that he could not afford to wait any longer and decided to join up with the *Chicago* and the *Perkins* before heading for a point further west where he could initiate air reconnaissance flights. It was therefore the original units, comprising TF17 plus the *Chicago* and the *Perkins*, which set off on a westerly course at 1800 on May 2, whilst still refuelling.

Fletcher's forces advanced slowly so as not to outdistance Fitch's

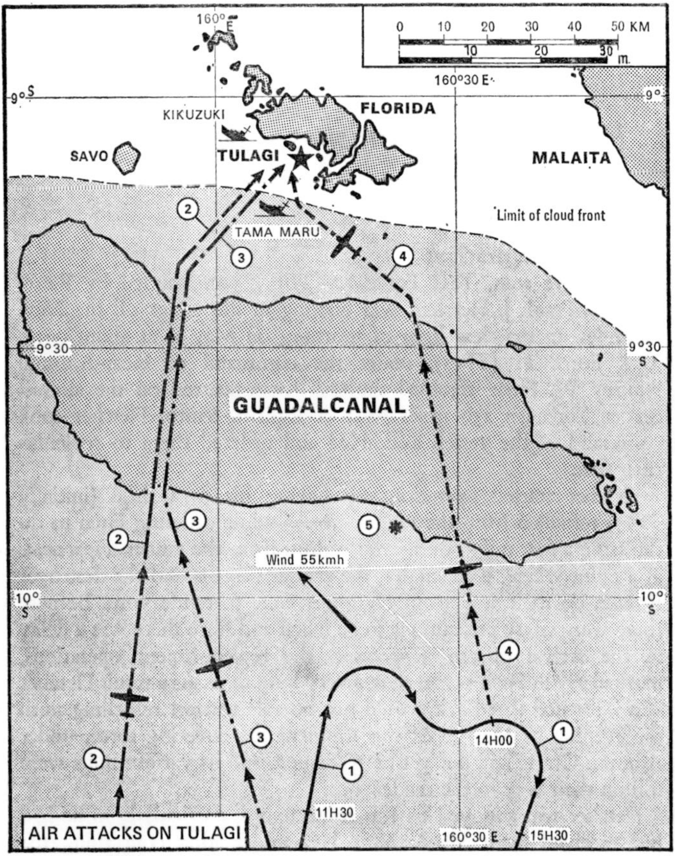

1 Course followed by Admiral Fletcher's Task Force 17
2 Flight course of first American air attack: Take-of at 0630 – Arrival at Tulagi 0815; Return 0930
3 Flight course of second American air attack on Tulagi
4 Flight course of May 3. American raid which took place during the afternoon of May 4. Take-of 1400 – Arrival 1515 – Return 1630
5 Point of forced landing of the 2 Wildcat fighters early in the afternoon of May 4

ships, with which he arranged to rendezvous at 15°S 157°E on May 4. Fletcher reckoned that his ships would then have been completely refuelled and that the position would be convenient for intercepting the enemy known to be approaching. It must be remembered that the Americans were convinced that the area of combat would certainly be in the region of the Louisiade Archipelago, since it was now known for certain that the Japanese objective was Port Moresby. Fletcher laid his plans accordingly, thinking that his adversary would be sure to pass through the Jomard Passage which was the only direct method of reaching Port Moresby discreetly from the north. This passage needed to be blocked from the south and with this in mind he sailed westward.

The two Task Forces were consequently progressing slowly west, still refuelling, and were about 100 miles apart. At eight o'clock on the morning of May 3 Fletcher had no idea of what Fitch was doing behind him; neither had he received any other news regarding the enemy. Careful to keep on the alert, he ordered the replenishment to be proceeded with, in particular the filling up of the destroyers which are liable to run out of supplies quicker than other types of vessels. In order not to give away his position to the enemy, Fletcher had ordered complete radio silence, so that, when Fitch had finished refuelling, at 1310 on May 3, ie. 24 hours earlier than he had expected, he was unable to contact Fletcher by radio and, for this reason, remained silent. This situation was highly regrettable and should have been allowed for in the general plan of operations since Fletcher would have certainly modified the latter if he had known Fitch's exact position. Fitch's silence is all the more incomprehensible because he could have sent off a weighted message by an aircraft, as is customary in such cases. However that may be, Fletcher was convinced that Fitch was still in the middle of refuelling, and May 3 passed therefore without any change in the arrangements previously made.

The light failed; night fell. Then, at 1900, a message from MacArthur's HQ set things in motion by stating that a reconnaissance aircraft based in Australia had flown over the southern Solomon Islands and spotted two enemy transports in the act of landing troops and equipment at Tulagi. Furthermore, numerous Japanese warships had been sighted north-west of this point and were beyond all doubt the force responsible for covering this landing.

The Tulagi affair

This was a real shock to Fletcher. The Japanese landing upset his pre-arranged plans, but, what was even more important was the fact that the threat was too immediate to be disregarded and that it represented the long-awaited news of preliminary movements on the part of the enemy. Also, this news was the first indication of the coming battle. Soon afterwards Fletcher received a new message from an Australian coastguard situated near Tulagi. This message, retransmitted by MacArthur's GHQ, stated that, at about eight o'clock that very morning, Japanese marines had taken Tulagi without opposition and that they had already set up a seaplane base there.

Finally MacArthur's reconnaissance aircraft had produced extremely significant meteorological information, viz. that a vast area of bad weather approximately 300 miles wide, was stretching from east to west, virtually cutting off Fletcher from Tulagi. More specifically, the southern limit of this bank of cloud was slightly to the north of the present position of TF17, while its northern limit almost coincided with Tulagi. This information threatened to prevent the carrying out of an idea which had just come to Fletcher's mind. This was to attack the Japanese bridgehead by air, but this bad weather, although providing excellent natural cover for his ships, might equally well impede his own pilots. The situation was precarious, since he could launch an attack only from the *Yorktown*, believing as he did that the *Lexington* was still being replenished. If he acted in this way, he would divide his forces and perhaps expose them to individual attacks by the enemy. On the other hand, if he did not intervene at Tulagi, he could expect within a very short time to be spotted by the seaplanes placed there by the Japanese.

On the principle that the best means of defence is attack, Fletcher decided to act. He had however to make certain arrangements and he decided to send the tanker *Neosho* escorted by the destroyer *Russell* to the rendezvous planned for eight o'clock on May 4 near the Willis Islands. In view of this change of plan and in order to warn the other vessels concerned, Fletcher arranged a new rendezvous for all his forces at a point about 300 miles south of Guadalcanal at dawn on May 5.

At about 2030 the *Yorktown* group sailed north at a speed of 24 knots, increasing to a speed of 27 knots, straight for Tulagi. As expected, the forces entered the area of bad weather, encountering frequent squalls with south-east trade winds blowing at more than 30 mph. The sea was rising and the night sky was almost entirely covered by huge black clouds. Under these very poor atmospheric conditions, Fletcher ran no risk of being spotted, and his ships sailed on all night at high speed unhindered. Nevertheless, the American admiral was still anxious, since if the northern limit of this bad weather zone did not remain near his objective as expected, his pilots would not be able to carry out the raid as planned. The *Yorktown* Task Group did not slacken speed however and arrived at 0600 at the pre-arranged point, 11°10′S 158°49′E, ie. about 100 miles south-west of Guadalcanal, where the aircraft were to be launched.

At about the same time, the tanker *Neosho* and the destroyer *Russell* had rejoined the *Lexington* group together with the vessels on their way from Australia commanded by Admiral Crace. It was not until this moment that Admiral Fitch was informed of Fletcher's new arrangements. The *Lexington* group was then too far off (about 250 miles) to support Fletcher, and Fitch decided to play a waiting game by continuing at low speed. Admiral Crace was awaiting Fletcher's return to retrieve the cruiser *Chicago* and reform his Task Force, Task Force 44 (TF44).

For their part, the Japanese had withdrawn their transports from Tulagi, once these were unloaded, and the covering forces of Admirals Goto and Marushige also had been withdrawing in the direction of Bougainville since eleven o'clock on May 3. All that remained off Tulagi were two destroyers and a few auxiliary vessels. As for the Japanese landing force intended for Port Moresby, this would not be setting off from Rabaul until 1800 on May 4. There were consequently only very few Japanese vessels within range of Allied reconnaissance planes during the morning of May 4.

At 0630 on May 4, a little before sunrise and in weather which was still cloudy, the *Yorktown* headed into the wind and launched her first aircraft, 11 Douglas Devastator aerial-torpedo carriers, followed by 28 Douglas Dauntless dive-bombers. The latter took off in two groups and each carried one 1,000lb bomb. A few minutes later they were followed by 6 Grumman F4F3 Wildcat fighters to provide air cover for the squadron. Captain Buckmaster had decided to retain his 18 fighters from Flight VF42 for defence and to launch them in three relays of 6 planes.

The Devastator torpedo aircraft and the Dauntless dive-bombers therefore set off for Tulagi without any fighter escort and flying in three separate groups. Lieutenant Commander Burch was in command of the first group of dive-bombers from Flight VS5; Lieutenant Short led the second group of dive-bombers from Flight VB5, while Commander Joe Taylor headed the 11 torpedo aircraft from Flight VT5. The planes flew through a mass of thick clouds interspersed at intervals with drops of rain. The sky seemed to darken steadily as they approached their target, but, as MacArthur's reconnaissance aircraft had reported, the weather rapidly improved and soon after eight o'clock the aircraft emerged into a clear sky immediately above Tulagi.

The first to arrive were, of course, the faster flying Dauntless dive-bombers. Commander Burch led them in a wide arc in order to identify their individual targets until, at 0815, he gave the signal to attack. One by one his bombers peeled off and zoomed down on the Japanese ships. The latter, whose officers were taken completely by surprise, had not yet reached full speed. One of the bombs grazed the destroyer *Kikuzuki* and damaged her badly enough for her crew to leap overboard. Two small minesweepers were hit severely and there was little doubt that they were beyond repair. Lieutenant Commander Taylor's 11 Devastators appeared at 0820 and came down almost to sea level before launching their torpedoes. Only one of the eleven scored a hit – on the minesweeper *Tama Maru*, which blew up. Ten minutes later, the second group of Dauntless bombers led by Lieutenant Short, arrived: they had in the meantime been on reconnaissance in the area, but the group drew blank and scored no hits.

The Japanese were clearly taken by surprise and they put up very little resistance. None of the American aircraft was hit by the enemy's anti-aircraft defences, and all had returned to the *Yorktown* by about 0930. The pilots, over-stimulated as they were after any raid, exaggerated their successes and transformed their insignificant triumph into a massive victory. Admiral Fletcher and Lieutenant Commander Pederson, who was in command of the *Yorktown*'s air groups, were wise enough to sift the truth from the 'chaff' of their pilots' contradictory statements and they decided to carry out a second raid. The decision to attack and thus take advantage of the enemy's discomfiture was soon made and the order to take off was obeyed so promptly that only a few pilots had the chance even to drink a cup of coffee. The aircraft, refuelled and re-armed, were already waiting with their engines turning over, and this second wave of aircraft flew off without incident.

This time there were 27 Dauntless dive-bombers and 11 Devastator torpedo carriers. They followed the same approach course and arrived above the target under the same conditions as their predecessors. This time the Japanese were on the alert and greeted the assault with a well-sustained fire from both ack-ack and machine guns. This did not deter the Americans however, and they had the satisfaction of damaging a Japanese patrol boat and destroying two seaplanes at their moorings.

Meanwhile the Devastators had launched their torpedoes, but without hitting their target. One Devastator was hit by anti-aircraft fire and limped away homewards, but soon lost height and came down in the sea. On their arrival back on the *Yorktown*, the American pilots declared that the results obtained had been 'sensational'. They also reported the presence of three other seaplanes at Makambo, a small island close to Tulagi.

Once more Admiral Fletcher suspected that their results had not been as brilliant as his pilots declared, but, without any means of checking their statements, he thought their exaggeration excusable. Indeed it is very difficult for pilots, during the inferno of combat below them, to get more than a brief view of their target; they have more than enough to do in attacking and at the same time protecting themselves from the enemy; they cannot be expected to study the operation objectively and in detail. Also, pilots are generally very young and allowance must be made for the enthusiasm of youth.

Fletcher was therefore not as satisfied as his pilots and, to get further tactical results, he decided to send them on a third raid, but on a smaller scale. They were merely to destroy the enemy seaplanes reported to be moored off Makambo. In the early afternoon, four F4F.3 Wildcats took off from the *Yorktown* and headed for Tulagi. They emerged from the clouds above the seaplanes' moorings and surprised the Japanese, who were not expecting another raid. In a few minutes, the three seaplanes off Makambo were destroyed and the American pilots then caught sight of the destroyer *Yuzuki* which was retiring from the action. The Wildcats made four machine gun attacks on the vessel and killed a number of the crew, including the *Yuzuki*'s captain. They were unable to destroy the vessel however, which sailed out of range.

Two of the Wildcats which had been hit by the Japanese defences,

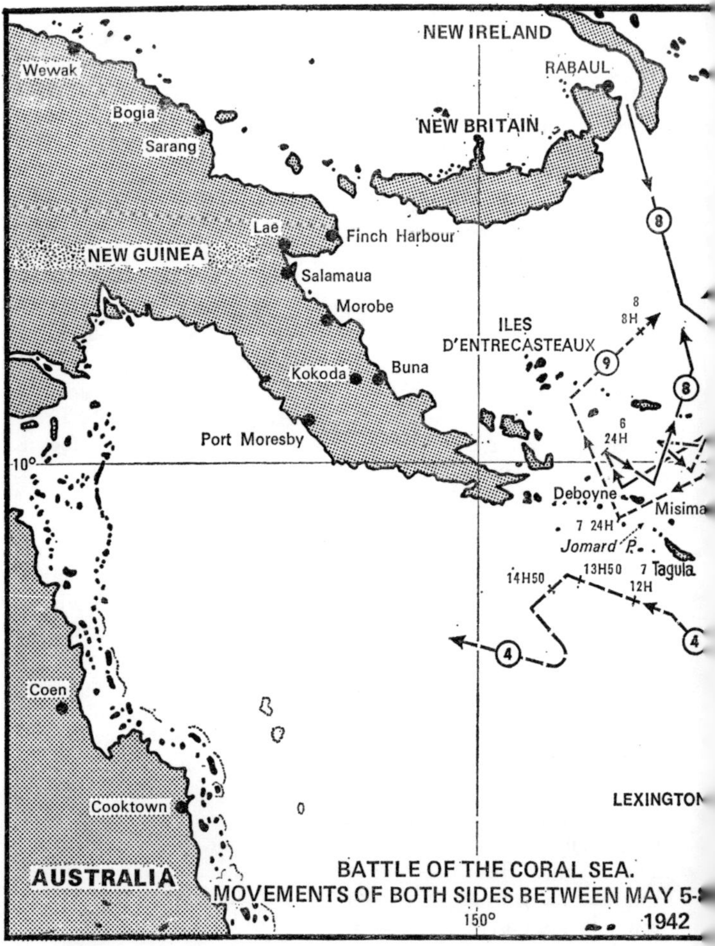

1 Course followed by Admiral Fletcher's Task Force 17

2 Course of Task Force 11 formerly under Admiral Fitch before they merged with Task Force 17

3 Course followed by the American tanker *Neosho*

4 Course followed by Admiral Crace's Task Force 44

5 Course followed by Japanese

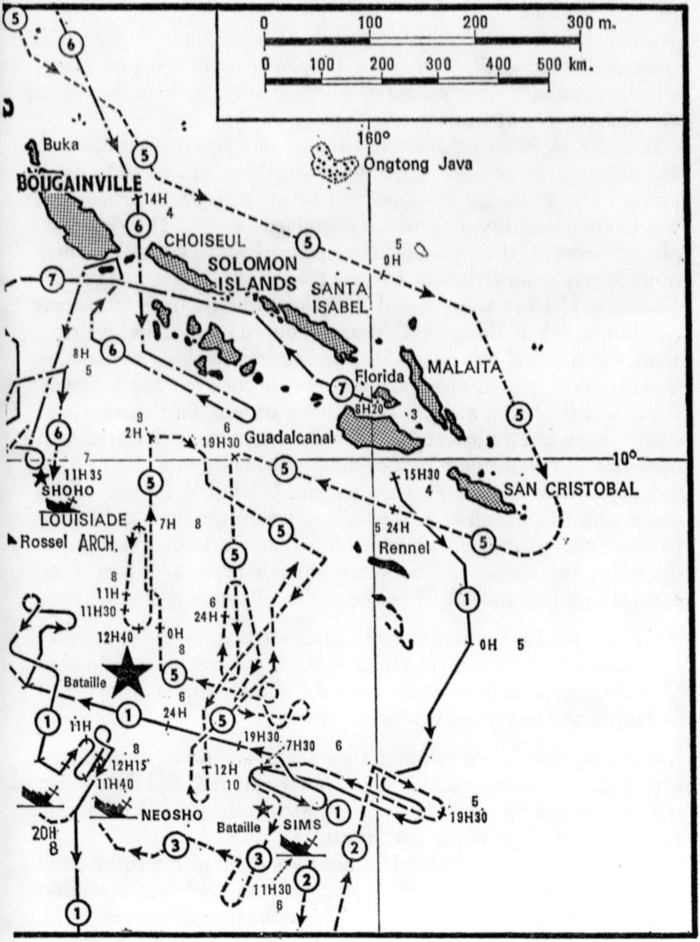

striking force under Admiral Takagi
6 Course followed by Admiral Goto's covering force
7 Course followed by Japanese naval force under Admiral Shima
8 Course followed by Port Moresby Landing Force
9 Course followed by support group under Admiral Marushige

gradually lost height and had to make a forced landing on the south coast of Guadalcanal. During the following night the two pilots, who were unhurt, were picked up by the destroyer *Hammann* which was able to venture inshore.

In order to finish off once and for all this Japanese bridgehead, and also to achieve some concrete results, Fletcher ordered a fresh group of 21 Dauntless bombers to take off at 1400. Their mission was to annihilate anything which resembled a target. The American planes discovered at Tulagi only four Japanese landing craft which they immediately sank. By about 1630 all the aircraft had returned to the *Yorktown*. Fletcher interrogated the pilots, studied their statements and eliminated anything which seemed doubtful. From his investigations, the Admiral was certain that the raids had all been remarkably fruitless. True, the Japanese had lost a few of their less heavy vessels, but their bridgehead had not been in any danger. Furthermore, the enemy now knew that at least one American aircraft carrier was operating in the northern part of the Coral Sea.

Scrupulously honest, Fletcher informed Admiral Nimitz of his action and its immediate results. The Commander-in-Chief of the Pacific Fleet once again showed himself to be both tolerant and generous. He blamed no one even though he would have been entitled to do so. Instead, he wrote in the following terms:

> 'This operation is indisputably disappointing in the quality of results achieved, particularly in view of the cost in ammunition and equipment. It shows the need for training in the dropping of bombs and torpedoes whenever possible.'

It is striking that, however bitter, these words are in no way intended even indirectly as a reproach. Nimitz knew only too well the relative weakness of the American Navy and, in particular, the lack of tactical training on the part of the aircraft carrier's pilots.

As we have seen, Admiral Fletcher took none of the enthusiastic reports of his pilots at their face value. He could only reach realistic results by sifting their statements. This estimate still proved to be more optimistic than the real situation warranted, and for this he could not fail to be held responsible. His over-estimate led him to signal to Admiral W. W. Smith, who was in command of the second group of heavy cruisers, asking him to detach two of his vessels on May 5 for the purpose of mopping up the remnants of the Japanese forces reported to be in the vicinity of Tulagi. The two heavy cruisers *Chester* and *Astoria* were detailed for this task, but Fletcher changed his mind and cancelled the order. In reality, Fletcher's reversal of his decision was due to the fear lest they should encounter other surface vessels, a situation in which the American Navy would be tactically inferior. It was also due to the arrival during the afternoon of a message relayed by MacArthur's headquarters reporting that a twin-engined B.25 Mitchell of the 90th bomber group had spotted an enemy naval force to the south of Bougainville, consisting of an aircraft carrier and two heavy cruisers. This squadron was none other than Admiral Goto's force which was patrolling the area. Fletcher's cancellation of his order had thus been a wise precaution.

Following the Tulagi encounter, the *Yorktown*'s task group headed first south-east, then south so as to rendezvous at the time originally arranged.

May 5 – A day of waiting

Meanwhile, the Japanese support group commanded by Admirals Marushige and Goto had withdrawn northwards and were too far away to intervene. Admiral Takagi's shock group was busy on May 4 refuelling in North Bougainville. News of the air-raid on Tulagi reached Rabaul very early in the morning, but owing to the complications of the Japanese radio communications Takagi was not informed until the middle of the day, just as his refuelling was completed. He headed south-east at a good speed, but by midnight he had only reached the northern tip of Malaita Island without encountering anyone.

On May 5 at 0815 at a point 15°S 160°E, the two American task groups joined forces. Fitch's and Crace's groups, who were on their way back from their waiting course to the southward, had meanwhile reversed course so as to make certain of being at the rendezvous.

The American admirals exchanged reports and drew up fresh plans. Then, at about eleven o'clock, the *Yorktown*'s radar detected an unidentified aircraft. As the cloud ceiling was very low, the American reconnaissance fighter was unable to sight his target, and so for the first time in the Pacific War, a Wildcat fighter was guided blind by the instructions of the radar control section on board the *Yorktown*. Knowing the heading and the relative distance, the American pilot was told in a very short time that he must be in the immediate vicinity of the target. At that moment, through a rift in the clouds, the fighter pilot caught sight of a large four-engined Kawanishi H6K *Mavis* seaplane which was quite close. At the Wildcat's second attack, the Japanese plane caught fire and plunged earthwards, burning like a torch. The encounter had been so short that the Japanese pilot had not had time even to call for help, much less to receive it.

At the HQ of the 25th air group in Rabaul, where the seaplane was based, it was assumed when it failed to return that it had been shot down, but as nobody knew its position, Admiral Inoue decided not to search for it, but to bomb Port Moresby as a prelude to the next landing. In the area of Port Moresby, the Japanese pilots based on the north coast of New Guinea were open to incessant attacks, and not a day passed without at least one and sometimes several aerial dogfights. Tirelessly the Japanese fighters from Lae, together with bombers from Buna, roared over the Allied stronghold which was continually receiving reinforcements from the reserve troops quartered in Australia and which was defended with such energy that it never succumbed as the Japanese hoped it would.

The American ships were then steaming through the large area of depression with little if any risk of being spotted by Japanese reconnaissance planes. Nevertheless, they were on their guard against any move the enemy might make. Their look-outs had been given strict instructions to remain on the alert and the fighter escort were overhead at all times. The three Task Forces TF11, TF17 and TF44 cruised south-eastwards, a little distance apart but well within range of visual signals.

Fletcher's naval group took advantage of this lull in proceedings to finish refilling the fuel tanks which the attack on Tulagi had emptied so considerably. In turn all the vessels steered a course parallel to the tanker *Neosho* and were replenished with fuel. Following their south-easterly course, the American vessels soon emerged from the area of storm clouds and entered the Coral Sea which lay, opalescent, basking in the sun. The sky was clear and blue and in it were scattered a few cumuli which a moderate trade wind from the south-east was speeding in the direction of the depression which the ships had so recently left behind them. Replenishment over, Fletcher decided to change course, and at 1930 all the vessels headed north-west. Convinced that the enemy would enter the Coral Sea by the Jomard Passage, Fletcher was anxious to take up a position which would bar the way to the Japanese invader.

By this time, the Japanese invasion fleet had left Rabaul and was making for the Louisiade Archipelago, accompanied by Rear-Admiral Marushige's naval support force. Admiral Goto's covering force was beginning to re-fuel from the tanker *Iro* at Shortland, south of Bougainville, while Takaga's striking force, having passed to the east of the Solomon Islands, was heading west in order to enter the Coral Sea. This fleet, at a speed of 25 knots, skirted Rennell Island on the north, and completed the Iapanese configuration. The pincers were ready to close on the American position.

Nothing particular occurred during this calm May 5 except that Fletcher received, both from MacArthur's HQ at Brisbane and from Nimitz at Pearl Harbor, secret messages which informed him that certain enemy naval groups were apparently converging on Port Moresby. The relative positions of these groups, which were still far apart from one another, had been such that Fletcher felt unable to intervene or even to send out reconnaissance aircraft.

In this context, we must remember that faulty administration was having a lamentable effect on American strategy at that time, namely the division, already mentioned, of the Pacific Ocean into command areas which were quite separate and so independent that no overlapping was allowed for. The south-west command area, under General MacArthur, covered three-quarters of the Coral Sea, so that all the manoeuvres connected with the coming battle were his responsibility. Although the purely naval aspect of the engagement planned had given Nimitz the right to preserve his seniority over Fletcher's group, this was the limit of his jurisdiction and produced a peculiar complexity in the use of aerial reconnaissance. At Noumea, Nimitz had available the supply vessel *Tangier* under the command of Commander de Baun together with 12 twin-engined PBY Consolidated Catalinas. These were too far away to reconnoitre effectively the southern Solomons, but could not be based elsewhere owing to the strict distinction between command areas. In fact, the greater part of the Coral Sea and its northern approaches were supposed to be patrolled by MacArthur's military aircraft, but his military aircraft were too few in number to take on such a huge task. Moreover, army pilots had not received any specific training for this, nor had they the highly specialised knowledge required for patrolling the ocean. These two circumstances were much to be regretted and created so great a gap in the Allied dispositions that Fletcher, who was sailing in MacArthur's command zone, was only partially able to fill it by using the carrier's reconnaissance aircraft, whose effective range was comparatively limited. It is true, of course, that military aircraft had already done a good job by providing Fletcher with useful information, but the aerial nets spread by MacArthur had far too wide a mesh to prevent every message from slipping through them. Nimitz and Fletcher were well aware of this problem and were justifiably anxious. Their anxiety was even more justified by the knowledge that reports from MacArthur's reconnaissance planes were sent to Brisbane for co-ordination and were then sifted so that only those 'considered to be useful' reached Fletcher's group. Happily, American radio-communications were very good, but, even so, Fletcher's ships lacked the support of long-range reconnaissance aircraft, which the Japanese were using to a considerable extent.

May 6 – Blind man's buff

At sunrise on May 6 there was a general feeling that something was about to happen. This feeling owed more to hypothesis than to certainty, but both Americans and Japanese shared a belief that a tactical engagement would take place before the day ended. Early that morning, Admiral Fletcher decided to carry out the orders given him on May 1 to form a single naval group from the total of vessels available to him. This unified Task Force was assembled at 0730 and was registered in place of Fletcher's former TF17. The operations of these numerous vessels were too much for Fletcher to control single-handed, and he therefore decided to delegate responsibility for air operations to Rear-Admiral Fitch, whose experience in these matters was considerable. As we shall see, however, he waited for a very long time before informing Fitch of his decision.

Meanwhile, on the same day, Admiral Goto's covering force, having finished refuelling at Bougainville, had headed south-west at 0830. The aircraft of Vice-Admiral Takagi's striking force were then situated to the west of Rennell Island, ie. north-west of Fletcher's group.

This powerful show of Japanese force thus seemed likely to stand in the way of any American move. At 0930 Takagi decided, on the strength of an unconfirmed report from Rabaul, to head due south in search of his adversaries. This was intended to cut off a possible American naval attack, and, being unknown to the Americans, might have had disastrous consequences for them. Takagi, who thought that the Americans were farther west, considered that, if they refused combat, they would flee in an easterly direction and would thus run into the arms of Goto's covering force which constituted the other half of the Japanese pincer movement.

Although without reconnaissance aircraft, Fletcher was not entirely without information. On the morning of May 6 he received a fairly large number of messages which, although not accurate or confirmed, suggested that the general movement of the Japanese towards Port Moresby was taking shape. Several reconnaissance aircraft took off from the American aircraft carriers during the morning, but none of them reported any signs of movement. The pilots who were reconnoitring the northern sector, reached the end of their radius of action only a few miles from Takagi's leading vessels, but without seeing them.

On the other hand, although the Japanese sent out no reconnaissance aircraft from their aircraft carriers (why this was so is a mystery), a Japanese reconnaissance seaplane from the *Yokohama* division at Rabaul spotted Fletcher's ships about eleven o'clock and reported their precise position. The message reached Rabaul before noon, but, owing to a succession of delays in re-transmission, it reached Takagi only the following day. It is clear that, had Takagi received the message at the beginning of the afternoon as might have been expected, he would have caught Fletcher in the middle of refuelling, when he would have been extremely vulnerable.

About noon, Fletcher received a signal from MacArthur's headquarters, informing him that at 1030 four B.17 flying fortresses had spotted and bombed the aircraft carrier *Shoho* from Goto's group, 60 miles south of Bougainville. The attack was abortive and the B.17s[1] had to retire in face of a violent counter-attack by the *Zero* fighters from this carrier. Some time later, another message from the same source indicated that reconnaissance aircraft had spotted a hostile naval convoy at 1300 south of Rabaul, heading southwest.

Although Takagi was still in the dark, Inoue knew that two of his squadrons had been discovered, that a relatively large American naval force was in the Coral Sea, and that air attacks would in all

[1] These four-engined B.17 bombers belonged to the 435th Squadron of the 19th Bomber Group based at Cloncurry in Australia. This group formed part of the Allied Air Force Division under Lieutenant General George H. Brett.

probability take place on the following day. Trusting in his power and certain that Operation *MO* would succeed, Inoue issued an order to continue operations as arranged at 1520.

In the afternoon of May 6 the situation became clearer. Fletcher had been warned of the presence of three Japanese aircraft carriers south of the Solomons and that the Japanese landing operation on Port Moresby was intended to set up in passing a seaplane base on one of the islands in the Louisiade Archipelago. He learned also that the landing party would pass through the Jomard Passage on May 7 ready to attack its target on May 8.

Admiral Takagi followed a course due south until the end of the afternoon, but, not having discovered anything and not having any precise information, he decided to turn back in order to start refuelling. When the Japanese striking force changed course in position roughly 13°20′S and 157°40′E, to was no farther than 70 miles from Fletcher's ships, but neither force knew that the other was so close. It was therefore by pure chance that the main action did not take place in the evening of May 6. After having changed course, Takagi's fleet turned north again at low speed and refuelled.

Since, as we know, Fletcher was ignorant of the position of the large Japanese aircraft carriers, he decided to take up a position south-east of Port Moresby so as to bring the Japanese landing-force vessels within range of his carrier's aircraft. Having spent the greater part of May 6 in refuelling, while steaming south-east at low speed, a course which was useful for the refuelling operation but which was at the same time leading him away from the enemy, Fletcher stopped replenishing at about 1800. An hour and a half later, at 1930, he headed north-west at a good speed, in order to reach the point where his aircraft were to take off by dawn on May 7. The tanker *Neosho*, now almost completely empty, and the destroyer *Sims* were then given the order to head south and rendezvous at a new position called *Rye* situated 16°S and 158°E by 1810 on May 7.

The American carrier's aircraft, which took off during the afternoon of May 6, flew over Takagi's striking force. They failed to see it however because at that moment it was below the thick layer of clouds forming part of the deep depression. The Japanese files indicate that the humming of the American aircraft was clearly audible on board the aircraft carrier *Zuikaku*. May 6 was thus spent in a game of blind man's buff based on information supplied by third parties. The tension was mounting on both sides, and one need not be a great strategist to realise that the following day would be one of significant tactical operations.

At midnight on May 6 the situation was as follows:

The Japanese striking force, which was steaming north while refuelling, was drawing away from the American ships. The Japanese invasion force was approaching the island of Misima, at the northern end of the Jomard Passage. Admiral Goto's covering group was situated north-east of the island of Deboyne. It should be noted incidentally that the light aircraft carrier *Shoho*, belonging to Goto's group, had provided cover throughout May 6 and, until night fell at 1815, for the Japanese naval forces. This was in order to protect the left flank of the Port Moresby landing group. This 12,000-ton aircraft carrier had received orders during the night of May 6–7 to take up a waiting position 90 miles north-east of Deboyne Island. Her aircraft were to be launched from that point at dawn on May 7. Lastly, Rear-Admiral Marushige's support group had reached Deboyne Island during the afternoon. The Admiral had then detached the seaplane refuelling tanker *Kamikawa Maru* with instructions to set up the naval air base planned. He had then withdrawn in a north-easterly direction to the Entrecasteaux Islands.

Meanwhile, Fletcher's ships were still sailing east-north-east straight for the south-east tip of New Guinea. It will be remembered that Fletcher's aim was to reach a point 310 miles south-east of Deboyne Island by dawn on May 7.

It should also be remembered that this Wednesday, May 6, 1942, was marked by the Allied announcement of very bad news: at Corregidor General J. Wainwright had capitulated, which involved the surrender of all the American forces in the Philippines. Happily this sad piece of information did not affect the morale of the Allied forces which were currently in the Coral Sea.

May 7 – Mistakes

It is difficult to ascertain today for certain whether the message received at Rabaul before noon on May 6 and re-transmitted to Takagi reached the latter before or after two o'clock in the morning of May 7. Rear-Admiral Hara, who commanded Takagi's aircraft carriers, states that at that moment he was guided by inspiration rather than by information sent on from Rabaul. However that may be, Hara succeeded during the night of May 6–7 in convincing his senior officer of the need to interrupt the refuelling operation and to head south. Hara's reasoning was based on the probability of American vessels being in the vicinity, as well as on the fact that it was essential to spot them and destroy them before turning west to support the landing force. Hara, therefore, asked to be allowed to take up a more southerly position from where, at dawn on May 7, he could carry out aerial reconnaissance to guard against attack from the rear. This was a wise move and it had the good fortune to appeal to Takagi who was still eager to know the exact position of the enemy.

Thus, at about two o'clock in the morning, the striking force changed course once again and headed south at a good speed. When day broke at six o'clock, several reconnaissance aircraft took off and spread out over the various search areas covering an arc from the south-west to the south-east. Admiral Hara was very pleased to have won his case and was delighted to be able at last to make full use of his aircraft. Incidentally, he stated after the war that during that night he had felt a kind of premonition which made him almost certain that the enemy was near. After the departure of the reconnaissance aircraft, silence fell again over the Japanese aircraft carriers which were anxiously awaiting news from their aircraft. An hour and a half went by without even the briefest of messages being received, and Admiral Hara was beginning to regret his action which would have considerably delayed Operation *MO*. He even feared a reprimand from his senior officer. Then, at 0736, a message was received by *Zuikaku*'s[1] radio. The message came from the aircraft assigned to the search area which was farthest east, and reported the presence of one aircraft carrier and one cruiser. The Japanese pilots, just like the Americans, sometimes seriously overestimated the forces spotted. In this case the vessels consisted solely of the tanker *Neosho* and its escorting destroyer *Sims*.

On the strength of this information, Admiral Hara immediately prepared for attack, increasing the speed of the squadron in order to cover the distance more quickly. On board both the *Zuikaku* and the *Shokaku*, mechanics were busy preparing the aircraft, refilling them with fuel and ammunition. Then one solitary aircraft took off in order to take up the contact which the first reconnaissance aircraft had been unable to keep for long because of its limited operational radius. A prodigious effort was made to hasten the preparations for

[1] Like almost all Japanese warships, Admiral Hara's two aircraft carriers had poetic names. *Shokaku* means 'flying heron' and *Zuikaku* 'joyous heron'.

the first wave of attacks. The first group of aircraft, consisting of 14 Nakajima B5N (*Kate*) bombers, flew off at about 0810, followed a few minutes later by 10 more. As they came up in the lift from the hangars on the lower deck, the Japanese aircraft were prepared for successive waves. The first wave consisted of 25 *Kate* bombers, the next of 18 Mitsubishi A6M (*Zero*) fighters and the third of 36 Aichi 99 D3A (*Val*) dive-bombers led by Commander Kakuichi Takahashi.

During this morning of May 7 all Japanese bases had sent out several reconnaissance aircraft in order to reconnoitre a wide strip of the northern Coral Sea. From the Japanese cruisers at sea, from Rabaul, from Shortland, from Tulagi and Deboyne, Japanese aircraft had set off to search for the Americans suspected of being in the area. The members of Admiral Inoue's staff were eager to locate the enemy in order to eliminate them as quickly as possible and thus carry out Operation *MO* with impunity. It was essential for the American presence to be revealed so that the Japanese could feel free of the threat they posed to their objectives. The means they employed were such that they could not fail to be spotted, and the first report of contact was signalled at 0840. It came from a small reconnaissance seaplane catapulted into the air by the cruiser *Kinugasa*. The pilot, no doubt elated at his discovery, got his co-ordinates mixed up and at Rabaul people had difficulty in understanding him. Nevertheless the message indicated that an enemy naval force of one aircraft carrier and ten other vessels was only about 200 miles south of the *Kinugasa* and 280 miles north-west of the last known position of Admiral Takagi's striking force.

As always, the signal was re-encoded and re-transmitted to the commander of the striking force. He received it only at about nine o'clock however, considerably later than the departure of the last aircraft of the Japanese attacking waves.

Admiral Hara realised to his chagrin that he had been too precipitate. Now deprived of the greater part of his fighter planes, he was no longer in a position to attack a new naval group of enemy vessels. Incidentally, contrary to what one might think, it is always very difficult to divert a group of aircraft which is heading for an already specified target. The pilots are prepared for a certain kind of attack with specific instructions and data relating to course and navigation, while the aircraft have been armed with carefully adjusted missiles. To divert this force in full flight, especially when it consists of an attacking wave of a carrier's aircraft, involves increased fuel consumption, which naturally reduces each aircraft's operational radius and upsets the pre-arranged plan often to the detriment of efficiency, not to speak of the confusion created by a collective change in course announced merely by radio. For this reason it is seldom that an officer in charge of carrier aircraft operations will change the course or the target of an operational squadron.

Admiral Hara was thus forced to hope and pray that Takahashi would destroy the first target in good time and return soon enough to refuel and set off again to attack this second enemy group.

The attack on the *Neosho*

At 0935, Commander Kakuichi Takahashi reached the position reported by the reconnaissance aircraft which had spotted the Americans that morning, but he found nothing but a deserted sea stretching out to infinity. Takahashi was very disappointed but almost at once he ordered several of his aircraft to fan out and explore a much wider surface of ocean. A few moments later one of his aircraft reported sighting one American tanker and one American destroyer, but no aircraft carrier. Takahashi instructed them to search and when this proved vain, he gave the order to attack both enemy ships.

Some thirty minutes earlier, the Japanese aircraft sent out to re-establish contact with the enemy had indeed spotted the two American vessels, but, expecting to meet one or more aircraft carriers and their escorts, he had merely dropped one bomb as he passed, which missed incidentally, and then set off in pursuit of a larger quarry. He had not thought there was any point in reporting the contact with such a miserable target, consisting, as far as he was aware, of one tanker and one destroyer. When this bomb hit the water, producing a great column of foam, the destroyer *Sims* was steaming about a mile ahead of the *Neosho*. Both ships saw the Japanese aircraft and brought their respective crews to action stations, but did not alter course.

When, at about 0945, the first Japanese attacking wave appeared, both the American vessels were on their guard. The Japanese aircraft attacked at low level but none of their 14 bombs reached its target. At about 1030 the second group of 10 *Kates* dropped bombs over the *Sims* but the American vessel, despite the accuracy of the Japanese bomb aimers, made a rapid turn and succeeded in avoiding them.

About noon matters grew worse with the arrival of the 36 *Val* dive-bombers under Commander Takahashi. The *Sims* set off at maximum speed, made a wide turn to port and was soon on the port quarter of the *Neosho* with the idea of assisting her with anti-aircraft fire. The Japanese bombers split into three groups and attacked from astern.

Diving one after the other on the two American ships, the Japanese pilots soon landed three 500lb bombs on the *Sims*. Two of these bombs, which were of the armour-piercing type, entered the interior of the destroyer and exploded in the engine room, causing numerous casualties and destroying the vessel's power plant. Her guns thundered and her machine guns rattled, but without hitting even one of the Japanese aircraft. A few minutes later a loud explosion within the *Sims* broke her in two and she began to sink by the stern.

The crew abandoned ship, but when the sea reached the funnel a serious fire broke out which engulfed both the men and the remnants of the unfortunate destroyer. Later it was found that one of the leading signalmen on board the *Sims*, named R. J. Dicken, had managed to get hold of a damaged lifeboat and, after a long search, had discovered a mere fifteen survivors, some of whom were wounded.

Of course, the Japanese aircraft were not only engaged in attacking the *Sims*. At the same time they set upon the *Neosho*, that 'great old lady', as the American sailors affectionately called her. They only needed a few minutes to land seven bombs on the tanker plus eight more in her immediate vicinity. One of the dive-bombers, whether deliberately or accidentally is not clear, crashed on the *Neosho*'s stern and the petrol from its tanks immediately started a large fire.

Captain Phillips, who was in command of the tanker, then gave the order to assemble preparatory to abandoning ship. The sailors however, in a state of alarm and perhaps even suffering from trauma as a result of the attack and the sinking of the *Sims*, did not hear the word 'prepare', but proceeded straight away to abandon the vessel. Many of them leapt overboard, while others seized life-rafts and two of the ship's boats. Some of the men obeyed their officers and came back on board, but others were drowned or set themselves adrift on the rafts.

As the Japanese aircraft retreated, the *Neosho*'s navigator took the ship's bearings, but, doubtless owing to the confused situation and the traumatic condition of the crew, he made a bad error in his calculations. This had very serious consequences which we shall discuss later on. It should perhaps be added that the attack on the two American ships and the destruction of the *Sims*, both deplorable, had a fortunate outcome in that these two ships occupied the attention of the Japanese carrier's aircraft, an unintentional diversion which enabled Fletcher to operate unopposed.

Crace's resourceful diversion

We have seen that since the evening of May 6 Fletcher's Task Force 17 had steered a course west-north-west in order to approach the focal point of the Japanese strike in the direction of Port Moresby. At 0625 on May 7, Fletcher reached a point 115 miles south of Rossel Island, the most eastern point of the Louisiade Archipelago. At that moment he needed to make his decisions very swiftly, for he knew that the enemy naval forces would have to pass through the Jomard Passage during the day.

One serious problem remained to be solved however. If Fletcher were to pursue his course west in order to cut off this convoy, he would inevitably be drawing away from the Japanese covering forces. These included, it will be remembered, an aircraft carrier which had been reported by MacArthur's reconnaissance planes. On the other hand, to attack this aircraft carrier and with it perhaps the entire Japanese striking force, the position of which Fletcher did not know, meant leaving the door to Port Moresby wide open, and he had received specific instructions to defend Port Moresby.

At 0645 Fletcher took the bold course of splitting up his forces. He ordered Task Force 44, under the British Admiral J. C. Crace, to continue westward and thus block off the south exit from the Jomard Passage, while the remainder of his forces were to take on the Japanese aircraft carriers. In this, Fletcher was convinced that he was going to confront the bulk of the enemy forces, and he felt that the decision was wise because it gave him the opportunity to pursue two equally essential aims. Fletcher's plan was not without danger however, since by depriving himself of the services of two heavy cruisers, one light cruiser and three destroyers, he was considerably reducing the power of his anti-aircraft defences, which were of course indispensable in repulsing any probable Japanese air attacks.

Fletcher's bold temperament was that of a gambler, and as it turned out it played a significant part in this decision. Although it must be recognised that luck was smiling on him, it is also true that what proved in the end to be a fortunate decision might just as well have developed into a catastrophic error in strategy. In carrying out his orders, Rear-Admiral Crace continued heading on the same course, taking with him the cruisers *Chicago*, *Australia* and *Hobart* and the destroyers *Walke*, *Perkins* and *Farragut*. This last destroyer formed part of the normal escort accompanying TF17, but, at the moment of separation, Fletcher had assigned her to TF44 in order to increase Crace's resources in light ships in case TF44 should encounter a force of enemy surface vessels.

This separation of the American forces did not long remain unknown to the enemy. As early as 0810, a Japanese reconnaissance plane caught sight of TF44. This was a single-engined seaplane which carefully kept out of range of the light vessels' guns. Admiral Crace reckoned firstly that the Japanese aircraft must belong to the new base set up in the Louisiade Archipelago, and secondly, that enemy aircraft would doubtless not be long before taking action. These two assumptions were absolutely correct. Crace was of opinion that he would be attacked by Japanese carrier aircraft, which he, like Fletcher, thought to be positioned close by in the north-east. Crace was an excellent tactician and placed his ships in lozenge formation, which is the most effective method of warding off an attack from the air, while concentrating all guns on the attacking planes. He also increased speed to 25 knots. TF44 remained on its initial course and, about 0940, caught sight of a group of aircraft with various numbers of engines. Action stations were assumed, but the order was quickly revoked on seeing that the aircraft were American army planes flying north-east.

At about 1130, other American land-based formations were again spotted. Crace concluded that MacArthur was doing his best to support the Navy and he felt very grateful for these land-based pilots who were not trained for naval air actions but who were nevertheless doing their best to bring information and help to the fleet. A little before 1400, Grace's naval group had almost reached the position at which Fletcher had ordered him to lie in wait for the enemy, south-south-west of the Jomard Passage, when suddenly the look-out reported the approach of unidentified aircraft.

Meanwhile, in the enemy camp, Admiral Yamada, commanding the 25th Air Fleet at Rabaul, was eager to send off his land-based aircraft, but the information available to him was as yet insufficient on which to base with accuracy any large air operation. It is true that he had learned of the presence of at least one American aircraft carrier in the Coral Sea, but the position given by the reconnaissance aircraft concerned was not sufficiently clearly defined and it was also too far away for aircraft to be sent out. On the other hand, as soon as Yamada knew the position of TF44 which was heading for Port Moresby, he was convinced that he ought to concentrate his attack on this extremely inconvenient force. He reasoned that (a) this force was about to compromise, perhaps even to bar the way of his landing force, and (b) a Japanese reconnaissance plane had reported the presence of at least one battleship. In the absence of aircraft carriers, this Task Force was sufficiently large and menacing to form the main target of the air attacks planned. Yamada was convinced of this and he gave the appropriate orders. Mostly from Rabaul, and to a more limited extent from Buna, numerous waves of bombers and torpedo aircraft took off during the morning and headed for the Allied force which had been spotted at 0810.

These aircraft were quickly identified on arrival by Crace's lookouts as hostile. They consisted of all of 11 single-engined bombers. As soon as they came within the ships' range, they were welcomed by firing which was as rapid and concentrated as it was accurate. This reaction on the part of the Americans, which had clearly not been expected, dispersed the attackers and nullified their attacks. The Japanese pilots, particularly the land-based among them, had had such easy successes in the initial weeks of the war that they were not expecting any difficulty in this case. They were still carried away by the memory of the way in which they had so easily destroyed the two large British warships, the *Prince of Wales* and the *Repulse*, which had been literally blown to pieces off the coast of Malaysia on December 10, 1941. After that, nothing seemed impossible to the Japanese pilots, but the wall of fire and steel presented by Crace's ships in face of their attacks took the wind out of their sails, so to speak, and destroyed at one blow their aggressive pride. The bombers dropped their bombs rather at random and fled. This behaviour came as a surprise to the Allied sailors who were used to Japanese air attacks which were both furious and diabolically accurate.

The sky was hardly clear of these bombers, when the American radar indicated the approach of a new formation. This time the attack was made by 12 twin-engined Mitsubishi type 96 G3M (*Nell*) bombers in impeccable order. Admiral Crace kept his vessels moving at maximum speed and opened fire with his guns as soon as the range permitted it. The Japanese twin-engined planes came down very low and almost immediately launched eight torpedoes which the vessels avoided by violent manoeuvres. Four Japanese aircraft were shot down before they could launch their torpedoes; a fifth caught fire just as it was climbing away from its target after launching its torpedo.

The guns had hardly had time to cool before, almost immediately, 19 *Nell* planes based at Rabaul flew in to attack. This time, the Japanese aircraft were flying high, between 20,000 and 25,00 feet, and were about to carry out level bombing, a trick at which the Japanese were past masters. Again forced to make violent manoeuvres, Crace's ships succeeded in avoiding all the bombs dropped, although there were some near misses. The enemy bombers changed course and had soon disappeared over the horizon.

The American and Australian forces were congratulating themselves on a great success when a fresh formation of twin-engined aircraft, which were beyond all doubt hostile, approached. Once more the ratings leapt to their guns, but there was something rather odd about the outline of the three aircraft which arrived. There was no time to stand and stare however, for several bombs came dangerously near to the destroyer *Farragut*. The aircraft retreated, leaving a feeling of indignation among the Allied sailors. The planes had been American B.26 Martin Marauders! Both eyewitnesses and photographs taken by the aircraft themselves during the attack proved that they must have been the aircraft from the 19th Bomber Group based at Townsville in Australia. Full of bitter anger, Admiral Crace despatched a telegram of reproach to MacArthur's headquarters. An acrimonious dispute followed and regrettable words were exchanged.

However that may be, the repulse of so many Japanese air attacks gave ground for encouragement. Firstly, the Allied forces had grown more skilful in avoiding attack, since they had emerged intact from a furious engagement and had even shot down a few of the enemy's aircraft. The experience of earlier disasters was bearing fruit and also proving that ships of different nationalities could collaborate with great success as a cohesive and effective tactical naval force. The disastrous end of the ABDA fleet in the Java Sea had thus been an unfortunate episode but nevertheless had provided valuable experience. Also, Crace's mission had not been fruitless, since it had not only strategically blocked the Jomard Passage, an operation which was to have profound and decisive consequences as we shall see;

but it had drawn on itself the attacks of Japanese land-based aircraft, which enable Fletcher to be left undisturbed.

Of course, on their return, the Japanese pilots gave news of their magnificent victory in sinking a battleship of the *California* class, a cruiser of the *Augusta* class and putting another battleship of the *Warspite* class out of action. Once again, we must remember that these exaggerations were not deliberate distortions of the truth; they were the effect of excitement and euphoria which are inevitable during aerial combat. Amidst the confusion, the noise, the violence of attack and a field of vision which is often greatly restricted, pilots of any country frequently confuse the great plumes of smoke from the funnels of ships manoeuvring at high speeds with the results of direct hits and the indications of serious fires.

The Japanese radio got hold of these unverified reports and spread the news of a brilliant victory over the enemy's navy, a victory which was at least as spectacular as that which started the war and which was marked by the destruction of the *Prince of Wales* and the *Repulse*. This had a serious effect, in that the Japanese commanders at Rabaul took these reports at their face value and so failed to launch any further air attacks, since they considered that this Allied force had been annihilated. It certainly could not have been the few losses they had sustained which caused the Japanese naval commanders to leave this Allied force alone.

A chance but successful attack on the *Shoho*

Let us go back a short time to the morning of May 7, when the Allied naval forces split up. When Admiral Crace's TF44 had been ordered to steer west-north-west, Admiral Fletcher, with the bulk of TF17, changed course to starboard and headed north. A little before dawn, he sent out several reconnaissance aircraft and impatiently awaited the results while approaching the position where he expected to find the enemy.

Roughly at the same moment the Japanese light aircraft carrier *Shoho* turned into the south-east wind and flew off four reconnaissance aircraft. Five others were to take off half an hour later in order to cover the landing force as it passed through the Louisiade Archipelago.

TF17 heading northward soon entered the area of bad weather. The sea was rough and the south-east trade wind was blowing vigorously. The cloud ceiling was high enough however not to interfere too much with air operations. These providential atmospheric conditions enabled Fletcher to remain hidden for the time being. Indeed, in order to catch sight of him, a Japanese aircraft would have had to come down below the layer of cloud and would thus have been within the immediate range of the ships' anti-aircraft guns and the American fighter escorts.

On the *Yorktown*'s bridge, Admiral Fletcher was becoming anxious. With scarcely contained impatience, he waited for the first message announcing contact with the enemy. He knew that it was a test of speed between himself and the enemy and that the advantage would lie with whichever one discovered the other first. Fletcher was certain that the Japanese had sent out reconnaissance planes and he could not refrain from admiring his enemy's expertise, although he was not unaware that the Imperial naval pilots had long been trained in this sort of mission, and that his own forces lacked this experience. He could not stop wondering whether his own team would let him down at a moment when he had taken a considerable naval risk in detaching Crace's force.

It was in the midst of this perplexity that he received news which eased the tension. At 0815 an American pilot sent the following coded message:

> 'Two aircraft carriers and four heavy cruisers 10°3′N 152°27′E, a short distance north of the island of Misima.'

Fletcher who, together with his staff, had rushed to the chartroom, decided that this must be the Japanese striking force and plotted it 225 miles north-west of his own position. Eager to engage the enemy as soon as possible, Fletcher gave orders to follow a northerly course and to launch all strike aircraft as soon as the range had lessened.

In the briefing rooms the pilots received their last orders, together with tactical and meteorological information regarding their coming mission. On the decks and in the hangars, the flight deck mechanics were filling the planes with fuel and ammunition and securing the bombs. The first aircraft were launched by the *Lexington* at 0925. Shortly before ten o'clock the *Yorktown* followed suit and, by 1030, 93 American aircraft had taken off and were already heading for the enemy's position. Between them the two American aircraft carriers retained 47 aircraft, mostly fighters, for their own protection. To launch its aircraft, TF17 had reversed course to head into the south-east wind, and at 1030 it resumed its northerly course and was again steaming under the natural cover provided by the area of bad weather. The clouds were even more dense and the wind was squally. It was soon necessary to turn again in order to recover the reconnaissance aircraft which returned a short time after the departure of the striking force.

When the pilots reported the result of their reconnaissance, it was clear that a serious error had occurred, not only in identifying the enemy ships which had been sighted, but also in the coded transmission of the message reporting this. In the light of eyewitness reports, the correct message now signified not 'two aircraft carriers and four heavy cruisers', but 'two cruisers and two destroyers'. Disappointment was intense, for the Japanese squadron which had been sighted was not Takagi's as Fletcher had thought. It was not even Goto's, which would have been almost as good a target; it was Marushige's, which in no way justified the use of the great fleet of aircraft which had been sent out.

Fletcher was distressed at this mistake and the deplorable consequences which it could not fail to have. As yet he was unaware that his Japanese opposite number was about to fall victim to a similar error by sending off all his aircraft to attack the tanker *Neosho* and the destroyer *Sims*. Fletcher's situation was all the more awkward because, for the same reasons as those affecting the Japanese, he was virtually unable to recall his aircraft. One faint hope remained however: it was possible that the bulk of the enemy fleet might be discovered in the interim. Fletcher clung to this idea as to a lifeline in the delicate and unfavourable situation in which he now found himself.

The admiral was also worried by the knowledge that he had been spotted before catching sight of the enemy's main fleet. At about 0820, a Japanese reconnaissance seaplane had been intercepted quite close to TF17 and there was no doubt that the Japanese pilot would have had plenty of time in which to report this contact before he was shot down in flames. Fletcher's assumption proved correct. At 0830 Japanese Headquarters were in possession of the exact position of the American carriers. In anticipation of an attack by the American Task Force, Admiral Goto had the *Shoho*'s aircraft made ready.

Despite the advantage which was at that moment with the Japanese, Admiral Inoue at Rabaul was acutely anxious. Attacks were being prepared for the very near future on the area around the

Louisiade Archipelago. The presence of Crace's force between Port Moresby and the Jomard Passage however, obliged him to make an extremely important decision. Fearing for the safety of the landing forces, at nine o'clock Inoue gave orders temporarily to reverse course. He instructed the group of supply vessels to wait north of the Passage and make sure that the battle was over and the enemy defeated before resuming its course for Port Moresby. This was the second fortunate outcome of Fletcher's decision to separate his forces into two, since it caused the enemy command to change its plans. We must remember that Inoue had not yet received the extravagantly lyrical reports of the attacks by land-based aircraft from the 25th Group. It was therefore due merely to the presence of this naval force that he was afraid, that he believed the projected landing was in jeopardy and that he finally made this significant decision. The Allies, of course, knew nothing of the revised Japanese plans and were therefore unable to profit from them. As we know, the Allied situation was a critical one, but at that moment an opportunity was vouchsafed them.

Lieutenant Commander W. L. Hamilton, chief of the VB2 flight belonging to the *Lexington*, observed something which would minimise the error due to the first message received and the resulting loss of time. In his SBD Dauntless, which was heading the attacking air squadrons, Hamilton flew over the island of Tagula at about 1015 and continued northwards in search of the enemy fleet which had been reported. Whether he deliberately deviated from his course, or whether he was carried off it by the wind without realising it, is not known, but, at 1022, Hamilton spotted from a height of 9,000 feet a large naval force amongst which he caught sight of what was indisputably an aircraft carrier. This was Goto's fleet, and the aircraft carrier was the *Shoho*. Hamilton immediately passed on his fortunate discovery and led the American formations to this new and particularly providential target.

Commander W. B. Ault, head of the *Lexington*'s air group, arrived on the scene thirty minutes later with two of his section leaders and confirmed the report of the original contact. Below them the Japanese ships had begun to twist and turn, and two *Zero* fighters took off from the *Shoho*. Before these two aircraft had time to intercept them, the three American planes dropped their bombs, but unfortunately without any of them hitting the target. However, one of them fell in the immediate vicinity of the aircraft carrier, and its blast knocked over five Japanese aircraft which were parked at the rear of the flight deck. A third *Zero* managed to take off at this moment and join its two fellows which were already engaged in an extremely unequal struggle. All three plunged courageously into the fray regardless of the consequences. In pursuing the American planes even into their dives and with complete disregard for their own anti-aircraft fire, the three Japanese pilots attempted to divert the dive-bombers from their target. They then launched a low level attack on the torpedo aircraft. Rocketing upward again as each new group of American planes arrived, the three Japanese pilots achieved some success but were unable to stem the tide.

Lieutenant Commander Hamilton, who had meanwhile assembled his group, led them into the attack at 1110 and his 10 Dauntless bombers dropped at least two 1,000lb bombs on the *Shoho* which caught fire and stopped. About 1115, the TBD Devastator torpedo aircraft from the *Lexington* launched low-level torpedo attacks under excellent conditions, but it was impossible to see how many of their missiles reached the *Shoho*. At 1125 came the turn of the *Yorktown*'s air group. New hits were registered on the Japanese light aircraft carrier which, by 1130, was already a mere piece of wreckage ravaged by flames and internal explosions. It was estimated that 13 bombs and seven torpedoes had hit the *Shoho* during the operation. The *Shoho*'s log, which was saved, shows that by that time everything on the aircraft carrier had been destroyed by enemy bombs or by exploding fuel tanks and ammunition stores. The order to abandon ship was given at 1131, and, at 1135, the *Shoho* went down in position 10°29′S 152°55′E.[1] The destroyer *Sazanami* managed to pick up only 100 survivors of the *Shoho*'s crew. Of the 21 aircraft normally carried on board the *Shoho*, 18 had been destroyed. The three aircraft which were still intact made for Deboyne Island, near which they landed. The pilots were recovered by landing-craft from the supply ship *Kamikawa Maru*, as their aircraft sank.

During the entire engagement, the American forces had known all the anxiety of actors on a first night, for this was the first time that aircraft carriers, or more specifically, their aircraft, were attacking Japanese adversaries of the same type. On board Fletcher's largest ships the Tannoy had been tuned to the frequency of the aircraft. Despite interference and spurious signals caused by the poor atmos-

[1] The loss of the *Shoho* is given in Japanese files as 0930 (Tokyo time) on May 7.

pheric conditions, the sailors had been able to hear the orders and ejaculations exchanged by the pilots. They had vaguely followed the course of the operation, but were unable to deduce what was really happening from the distorted sounds emitted by the loudpeakers. Suddenly, about 1130, the cracklings ceased and the voice of Commander R. E. Dixon, who commanded the VS2 flight and who was well known to the *Lexington*, was clearly heard saying a phrase which has become famous:

> 'Scrub one flat-top! [1] Dixon to aircraft carrier: I repeat: Scrub one flat-top!'

On receipt of this message, the atmosphere immediately relaxed on board the American ships which were in position approximately 100 miles south-east of the scene of this engagement. Of the 93 aircraft which took part in this attack, only three were lost, and, at 1335, the remaining 90 were back on board their respective aircraft carriers. From the evidence of the pilots, who reported the presence within the same enemy squadron of four heavy cruisers and two destroyers, a second attack was prepared and the aircraft were ready to take off again at 1450.

Fletcher was obviously tempted to follow up his success. He refrained from doing so however, because he felt that these targets were not worth the risk of having his own aircraft carriers deprived of aircraft should the opportunity of striking at the large Japanese aircraft carriers present itself. Incidentally, his prudence was justified by the announcement of the attack made by the Japanese carrier aircraft on the *Neosho* and the *Sims*. The captain of the unfortunate tanker had broken radio silence in order to warn Fletcher of this attack and signalled that he was 'as full of holes as a colander'. The *Neosho* was only just keeping afloat thanks to the air trapped in her empty tanks. The navigation error made by the *Neosho*'s navigator placed the tanker at a point some way to the east and suggested therefore that Takagi's fleet was more to the eastward than it really was.

Fletcher's third worry was not having yet spotted the large enemy aircraft carriers whereas his own position was precisely known to the Japanese. Moreover, to send off a large air formation at this time would be to force his pilots to return at nightfall, perhaps even in the dark, and he was not willing to present them with the extremely

[1] 'Flat-top' is the nickname given by Americans to their aircraft carriers.

difficult task of a night landing, in addition to the fatigue they must be feeling after two successive raids and probably with damaged aircraft into the bargain.

Operation *MO* in jeopardy

It will be remembered that, on the Japanese side, Admiral Inoue had instructed the landing force, at nine o'clock on the morning of May 7, to reverse course temporarily. Quite simply, this was an order to make a provisional retreat which was supplemented in the afternoon by an order to head for Rabaul. In order to minimise the effects of this decision in the eyes of his superiors, Inoue stated that the landing at Port Moresby should be delayed 48 hours owing to certain tactical considerations. There was no doubt however in Inoue's mind, and, about midnight, he detached two battle-cruisers from Goto's group ordering them to rendezvous with and reinforce Takagi's striking force.

If Inoue's intention had really been to resume his course towards Port Moresby, he would not have stripped the convoy of its escort. On the contrary, he would certainly have reinforced it to meet the threat posed by the American presence in the vicinity of the Jomard Passage. There is no doubt that Admiral Inoue was being over-cautious, but the loss of the aircraft carrier *Shoho* had affected him considerably both as a symbol and a warning. The only offensive operation Inoue had in mind was to attack the American naval forces at night with surface ships. In the evening, therefore, he ordered Goto's cruisers and Kajioka's destroyers to regroup in the vicinity of Rossel Island before attacking the Americans with guns and torpedoes. It is probable that by that time Admiral Inoue had no faith in this idea himself because, at about midnight, he cancelled his order, reassembled the ships which had been detached and, as we have just seen, sent two of Goto's cruisers to Takagi.

MacArthur's aircraft, which had tirelessly continued their reconnaissances on Fletcher's behalf, noticed the Japanese invasion convoy change course and reported it. For a moment Fletcher could not believe it. It seemed to conflict with everything he knew of Japanese mental processes, and he could not bring himself to credit this information at all. Nevertheless, several observers confirmed this extraordinary report, and Admiral Crace was the first to be convinced by it. For him the loss of the *Shoho* would not have been enough in itself to justify this withdrawal, but its symbolic value and the defeat of the aircraft attacking his own ships must have made Admiral Inoue waver in his convictions. The British admiral therefore accepted the news as an astonishing but probable fact, but with some reserve. For all he knew, this unexpected move on the enemy's part might well turn out to be a trap, and it was advisable to be wary. He thus proceeded to check before passing his opinion on to Fletcher. About midnight, Crace's squadron was 136 miles south of the south-eastern tip of New Guinea, heading west, and the British admiral followed the same course during part of the night. He thus ensured that no Japanese movement could occur under the cover of night, but as no message was received to invalidate his information on the enemy's withdrawal, Crace reversed course and headed south in the direction of Australia as instructed in his orders.

In reality, Admiral Inoue was considerably abashed by the loss of the *Shoho*, since it was a loss that brought neither strategic nor tactical gains. What affected him most however, was the presence of Crace's squadron between his convoy of supply vessels and Port Moresby. Inoue was not expecting his adversary to divide up his forces and he knew the vulnerability of his supply vessels which would have no chance against an enemy squadron which had already exhibited so much toughness and determination during the recent aerial bombardments. The Japanese pilots had reported this squadron to be decimated, but it still had enough ships in fighting trim to threaten the invasion force. Moreover, Inoue believed from what his pilots had told him that Crace still had warships, against which his cruisers and destroyers would have very little chance. Again, Inoue resembled many of the Japanese leaders; he was disconcerted by American strategy which did not fit in with his reckoning nor with the course and intentions which he had ascribed to the enemy. The Japanese temperament is given to predicting what the enemy will do. If the enemy does not follow the course assigned to him, the Japanese find great difficulty in deviating from their pre-arranged plans and in initiating new military operations. Inoue found himself unable to carry out Operation *MO* to the letter, because the enemy had acted in a way that his plan had not foreseen. There was no point in pursuing the plan and it was better to wait. The simple fact of delaying Operation *MO* produced a pitiable psychological effect on the behaviour of the Japanese leaders who were baffled at this annoying hitch. As so frequently happens during wars, psychological factors played on this occasion a highly significant part.

Takahashi's nightfall raid

Let us go back a little to the afternoon of May 7. Admiral Takagi had been put out by the misinterpreted report of contact with the enemy, which had caused the take-off of his air group against the *Neosho* and the *Sims*. The destruction of the American destroyer and the damage caused to the tanker had in no way justified the air attack, particularly since he had learnt soon afterwards of the presence of an American aircraft carrier in the vicinity. Since he could not recall Takahashi, he had impatiently to await the return of his aircraft.

Before these aircraft were back on board, Takagi had received news of the attack on the *Shoho*, which proved that there was not merely one but two American aircraft carriers in the Coral Sea. His anxious expectancy developed into impotent rage, so that, when Takahashi landed, orders had already been given for the carrier's aircraft to be refuelled and rearmed. Nevertheless, both Takagi and Hara were anxious. A take-off at this time would mean that the aircraft would have to return in the dark, and this would make the task of the pilots, who were already tired after the first raid, particularly difficult. Furthermore, a take-off now would prevent the use of *Zero* fighters, which were not equipped for night flying. Takagi hesitated, but the prospect of attacking the American aircraft carriers at nightfall, and at a moment when the fighter escorts and carrier's anti-aircraft fire were impeded by the poor visibility, was too tempting.

It is clear that Takagi was in the same dilemma as Fletcher, ie. whether or not to launch a striking force at the end of the afternoon. While Fletcher refrained from doing so for the reasons given above, Takagi went ahead and gave the order irrespective of the problems thus created for his pilots. The flight leaders on board the Japanese aircraft carriers were asked to choose from among their junior officers all pilots with the greatest experience in night flying and also those who had the best night vision. As a result, it was the élite of the Japanese carrier pilots who took part in this attack. At about 1615, the pilots were ready and briefed as to the details of location, meteorological conditions, and the return course to be taken, while on the flight decks the engines of the leading aircraft were already turning over.

At 1630 Commander Kakuichi Takahashi took off again accompanied by 12 Aichi *Val* dive-bombers and 15 *Kate* torpedo carriers. Their journey was a long one and they expected to make contact with the Americans at about 1800, ie. shortly before nightfall. The weather had worsened, and the aircraft had to make their way through enormous cloud formations together with intermittent rain which made navigation difficult. The Japanese aircraft had frequently to change course. This again lengthened the distance to be travelled, and twilight came before they had reached the calculated point of attack.

At the very limit of his operational radius, Takahashi made one last search before giving up and issuing the order to return to the aircraft carriers. Takahashi was annoyed at not having been able to accomplish his mission and, like his men, he was feeling the effects of the cumulative fatigue resulting from two successive air attacks. A short time after turning for home, he gave the order to jettison the bombs and the torpedoes in order to lighten the planes, economise on fuel and make it possible to land without danger.[1] Night fell on the sea, and the Japanese aircraft split into three groups, each seeking its own direct way towards its mother ship.

Contrary to what Takagi and Hara were thinking, the American aircraft carriers were much closer to them, and Takahashi's aircraft had flown over an area which was more or less free of Allied ships. The pilots were however about to be bitterly disillusioned. After flying for some time in the direction of their aircraft carrier, the Japanese aircraft passed, without knowing it, very close to the real position of TF17. They were suddenly attacked by Wildcat fighters belonging to the last combat air patrol over the *Lexington* and the *Yorktown*. The battle was as short as it was violent, and took place in the pale light of the final rays of the sun reflected against the clouds. The Wildcats were particularly aggressive and shot down no less than eight *Kates* and one *Val* at a cost of two of their own, one of which was being flown by Ensign First-Class Paul G. Baker.

This aerial engagement had involved only one of the three groups of Japanese aircraft, but what happened to the other two would appear almost incredible, although the occasion has been thoroughly authenticated. The tired Japanese pilots, who were in all senses of the term completely in the dark, had roughly calculated their flying time for the return journey, and once they had reached this point they began to search for their aircraft carrier by describing concentric

[1] It was virtually impossible for an aircraft to land on its aircraft carrier still carrying its bombs or torpedoes, in view of the danger of explosions caused by the shock produced by the wheels hitting the flight deck.

circles of ever increasing radius. Several of them, who were more exhausted than the others, thought several times that they could make out the welcoming flight deck. At about 1900 three of them did indeed spot an aircraft carrier and began to descend. They lit their indicator lights and sent a series of flashlight signals.

On board the *Yorktown* everybody was, of course, extremely surprised, since all the aircraft were on board. Almost immediately however it was realised that the aircraft were hostile. The *Yorktown* replied obligingly to the signals, the flight deck landing lights were switched on and everyone prepared to welcome these invaders. Although they obviously did not understand the meaning of the signals emitted by the Americans, the Japanese pilots must have been fairly trusting in their attitude, because they throttled back and approached the aircraft carrier on the starboard side.

The pilot of the first Japanese aircraft passed under the bow of the *Yorktown* at the very moment when a gun flashed. For a brief moment the scene was lit up, and the pilot must have realised the terrible mistake he was making for his engine started to roar as he opened the throttle again to its maximum. The Japanese aircraft regained height followed by its two fellows and they disappeared into the night. On board the *Yorktown*, surprise was mingled with delight. Comments were rife, and the rating who had put the Japanese to flight was almost the subject of a grudge. The men were still talking about it when, at about 1920, the same occurrence was repeated. Three other Japanese pilots had caught sight of the little red lights which were left on to delineate the limits of the *Yorktown*'s flight deck and took them for the lights of one of their own aircraft carriers. The three pilots reduced speed, lowered their undercarriages and lifting flaps, and described a large circle to land along the axis of the runway. Obviously they intended to land, and, as before, the *Yorktown* replied to the flashing signals of the Japanese pilots.

The first aircraft was already at the final limit of its endurance and about 150 feet from the stern of the *Yorktown*, when it was surrounded on all sides by a hail of tracer bullets. In alarm, the Japanese pilot opened his throttle and climbed away. His two companions followed his example, but one of them, hit by the *Yorktown*'s anti-aircraft fire, came down in the sea a short distance away. Similar mistakes were repeated on various occasions during the Pacific War, but never in such numbers as on this, the evening of May 7.

In addition to the fatigue imposed on the Japanese pilots by the need to carry out two such long-distance raids in one day and return under the extremely difficult conditions of night, for some of them, it was the first time they had landed on aircraft carriers at night. To make matters worse, their carriers had no radar or any other direction-finding equipment, so that it was impossible for them to home their aircraft on their positions. Furthermore the Americans had managed to jam the frequencies on which the Japanese planes were transmitting. This meant that the radio-operators of TF17 were able to scramble any transmissions and interfere with reception over the enemy's entire network of communications, thus preventing the Japanese pilots from homing in on the precise bearings of their vessels. Admiral Hara was well aware of this, but could do nothing to ease the situation for his pilots. When he heard in the distance the engine noise of returning aircraft, he courageously ordered the flight-deck search-lights to be switched on despite the risk of his vessels being spotted.

The 17 planes surviving from the raid appeared, and all the pilots lost their heads and attempted to land simultaneously. This unusual breach of discipline was due to the fact that only a very few planes had more than a gallon or so of fuel in their tanks. The flight-deck officers had the greatest difficulty in enforcing their authority and suppressing this panic-stricken chaos. There followed some tense and dramatic moments, during which the pilots desperately competed with each other for landing positions. The night was too dark for anything to be seen except the beams of the searchlights and the position lights of the planes which were jostling with one another at very low heights. The disorder thus created could not but cause losses, and some of the aircraft crashed owing to lack of petrol, while others were forced to land extremely violently. Eleven aircraft were destroyed in this way, and, by 2100, only six planes had landed intact. This catastrophic outcome was particularly bitter in view of the negative results of the raid.

Reciprocal aims

After the two attempts by Japanese aircraft to land on the *Yorktown*, the Americans had endeavoured to follow their course, and at 1930 the *Lexington*'s radar screen picked up a number of aircraft which were wheeling above a point some thirty miles[1] away. This point

[1] This distance, which was calculated by the radar operators, turned out on investigation to be quite wrong. It was in fact much greater.

seemed to be the position of the Japanese aircraft carriers, and the radar operators on board the *Lexington* soon became certain that this bunch of aircraft flying at low speed must be the same as the one they had seen previously, which was now coming in to land on the carriers' flight-decks.

When informed of this extraordinary discovery, Admiral Fitch tried to contact Fletcher, but was unable to do so until 2200. This was due to difficulties in sending the low-powered transmissions required to prevent the enemy from learning by high-powered interception techniques how close the Americans were. When he finally received the message, Fletcher was sceptical, since his own radar had picked up no similar signals. This was not surprising in view of the time the enemy had had to increase their distance before Fletcher received the message. Fletcher's point of view was a reasonable one, since, at 2200, the Japanese aircraft carriers were 95 miles east of the *Yorktown*. However, he called his officers together and outlined the situation to them. Two possibilities were open to him: either to send a group consisting of cruisers and destroyers to attack the Japanese force, or to send this same group to carry out a night attack on Tulagi. Someone pointed out that TF17 would risk being deprived of its protective screen at day-break and that the outcome of these naval attacks was on the whole uncertain, particularly as the moonlight was very faint and was hardly conducive to good aiming. Fletcher was, incidentally, convinced that the following day would see the approaching confrontation between Japanese and American naval aircraft and accordingly decided not to allow his surface vessels to engage in night operations, but to keep them with him for his protection, particularly in regard to anti-aircraft defence. In his report on the operation, which was written somewhat later, he wrote:

> 'All in all, it seemed best to keep our forces concentrated and to prepare to confront the enemy's aircraft carriers on the following morning.'

As we have seen, Admiral Inoue also refrained from launching a similar night attack, but, what was even more curious, Takagi, whose pilots had reported the presence in the vicinity of the American aircraft carriers, had the same intention. Both Takagi and Hara were mortified by the day's failures and the loss of a considerable number of aircraft for nothing. Never had Japanese aircraft carriers gained so small a tactical advantage, and the idea on the part of both admirals of mounting a night attack by surface ships sprang from their desire to save face following their humiliation. The American aircraft carriers had been reported by reconnaissance aircraft to be between 40 and 60 miles[1] to the west. On board the heavy cruiser *Myoko*, Takagi discussed with his staff the possibility of attack, but his officers pointed out that he had only two heavy cruisers and six destroyers, while he was as yet unaware of the American force's exact strength. The discussion went on for a long time, but before any decision could be reached, a message arrived.

This signal came from Rear-Admiral Koso Abe, who was in command of the transports of the invasion force, and requested that the striking force should provide air cover at dawn on May 8. Takagi and Hara therefore abandoned their argument in favour of a night attack. After the war, Admiral Hara declared:

> 'We gave up the idea because our main mission, as defined in Operation *MO*, was to provide distant cover to the invasion force. This was for us all the more essential because we guessed that the following day would be the decisive one.'

On May 7, at about 2200, the Japanese striking force headed north and by midnight had reached a point 12°40′S 156°45′E. Almost at the same moment, TF17 headed south-west.

The two adversaries were thus heading away from each other; their commanders, however, although neither knew the other's position, were certain that the great confrontation would take place on the following day, May 8. Both Fletcher and Takagi were eager for the battle to come and they were not unaware that the advantage would be, as always, with the one who located the other first.

[1] This distance was also incorrect, but closer to reality than the distance given to Fletcher by Fitch. In fact the distance was between 90 and 100 miles.

CHAPTER THREE

The Battle of May 8 and its consequences

An equal struggle

The Japanese striking force followed its northerly course throughout the night of May 7–8, until at 0600 it was 100 miles south-east of Rossel Island, the point from which Hara had calculated his first daytime reconnaissance aircraft should take off. Before sunrise therefore, several Japanese aircraft took off with instructions to patrol an arc of 90° south-south-west (from 145° to 235°) on a radius of 200 miles. Following a tactical plan which was to become customary, the Japanese did not wait for the result of these patrols. Instead, at 0822, Commander Kakuichi Takahashi took off, leading 33 *Val* dive-bombers, 18 *Zero* fighters and 18 *Kate* torpedo aircraft. Takahashi had received orders to follow the axis of the arc of the initial patrols and to rendezvous immediately contact was established with the reconnaissance aircraft sighting the American aircraft carriers. However, the Japanese attacking squadrons broke up into several groups in order to assist the reconnaissance patrols. At about 0825, the striking force, which had in the meantime turned south-east in order to launch its aircraft, increased speed to 30 knots and steamed due south in the presumed direction of the enemy. In this way, Admiral Hara was cutting short the return journey for his aircraft, which would enable him to pick them up earlier.

At 0833, the first message reporting contact reached the *Shokaku*'s bridge. The message had been sent by Chief Petty Officer Kenzo Kanno, piloting a *Kate* and who, right at the end of his operating radius within the arc being patrolled, had discovered TF17. Kanno had calculated the exact position of the enemy force and also gave its composition, ie. two aircraft carriers and twelve escort vessels consisting of cruisers and destroyers. The message was immediately sent on to Takahashi who ordered all his aircraft to converge on the point indicated. The reconnaissance pilot took advantage of several clouds in which to hide and wait so that he could maintain contact

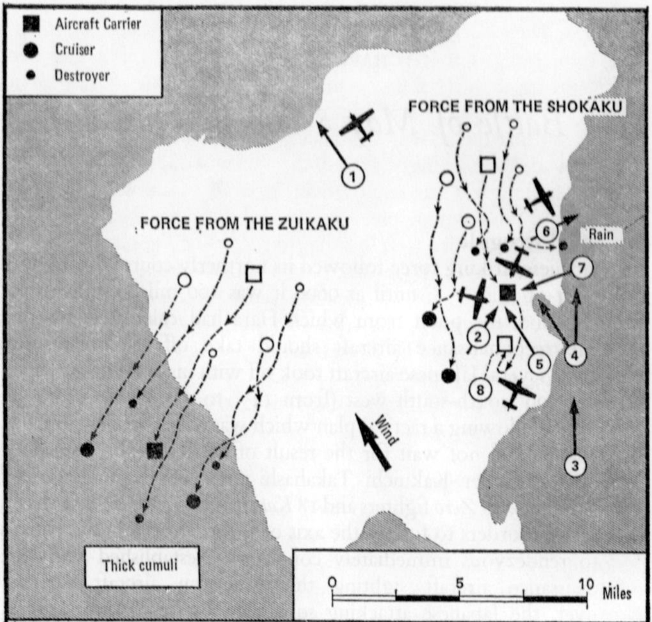

MOVEMENTS OF THE JAPANESE FLEET
BEFORE AND AFTER THE ATTACK ON MAY 8 1942

The blank symbols indicate the position of the Japanese ships at the moment when they were spotted. The filled-in symbols represent the same ships at the time when the Americans attacked.

1 Group of dive-bombers from the *Lexington* lost in the clouds before reversing course and returning to their carrier without attacking

2 Group of dive-bombers from the *Yorktown*

3 Attacking aircraft from the *Lexington*

4 Group of torpedo aircraft passing close to the Japanese Fleet without seeing it

5 Four Dauntless bombers from the *Lexington* attacking the *Shokaku*

6 The *Lexington*'s torpedo aircraft gathering in the clouds

7 The same aircraft attacking the enemy in their turn once they had spotted the Japanese planes

8 Position of the *Shokaku* after the attack when it had just received permission to return to Japan for repairs

for a few moments without being intercepted by the American defences. Nevertheless, having used up half his reserve fuel, Kanno was soon obliged to return to base. The Japanese pilot had been flying for some thirty minutes in the direction of his aircraft carrier when he perceived Takahashi's attacking force in the distance. Kanno felt that the attacking formation was not headed in the right direction and accordingly feared that they would waste valuable time in looking for the enemy fleet. It is also possible that he had doubts as to the accuracy of his report and therefore wished to make sure that his comrades were heading directly for the target. No one knows, but whatever his reasons, Kenzo Kanno turned and at the risk of his life, headed towards the American force in order to direct Takahashi's formation to it. Although he knew that he would no longer be able to regain his aircraft carrier, he carried out his mission to the end, heading the group attacking TF17. Having made this extremely brave gesture, he resumed his course towards the Japanese ships but soon ran out of petrol and went down with his aircraft far from all help.

On being awakened before dawn on May 8, Admiral Fletcher's first thought was to search for the enemy. His officers subsequently declared that the admiral had never been as aggressive as he was that morning. He was quite obviously tensed up and eager to establish contact with the enemy. The situation of the Americans however was not too favourable in these early hours of May 8. Although deprived of Crace's Task Force 44, the American group had certain advantages including radar and 122 aircraft available for combat. In this context, incidentally, it should be noted that on this occasion the possession of radar did not give the Americans any very great tactical advantage. Radar was only of use in the detection at short distances of Japanese aircraft. The aircraft strength on each side was almost identical in numbers (121 as against 122), but it was somewhat differently distributed. Although the Americans had a greater number of dive-bombers, the Japanese had an advantage in numbers of torpedo aircraft and fighters, in the use of both of which they were highly efficient.

Fletcher however was anxious on several counts with regard to the impending battle. He knew all too well that the enemy aircraft carriers *Shokaku* and *Zuikaku* had been working in 'double harness' for more than six months. This had given them a combined experience which was particularly dangerous as far as the *Lexington* and the *Yorktown* were concerned, since it was only the present circumstances which had brought these two vessels together. Moreover, the American admiral knew that his light anti-aircraft guns had not a good reputation amongst those who manned them. Finally, the course he had followed throughout the night had taken him out of the bad weather so that his ships were now in the full light of day under an almost clear sky.

The atmospheric conditions, which had up to then been in his favour, now seemed to turn against him. The Japanese only had to head south, Fletcher correctly presumed, in order to enjoy the protection of the same area of depression. Fletcher's worries were also due to his ignorance both of the enemy's position and the precise composition of his fleet. The few reports which had been received by his staff officers during the night were very inaccurate and mostly contradictory. At dawn therefore he proceeded to carry out a methodical reconnaissance over a large arc ranging from north-west to north-east so as not to be caught unawares by his adversary. Fletcher ordered Fitch to send off aircraft from the *Lexington* for this purpose. At dawn, about 0625, 18 Dauntless aircraft took off and spread out along several axes in the fashion of the Japanese but, of course, in the opposite direction.

It was more than two hours before Fletcher received any news from his reconnaissance pilots, and during that time he was steaming blind. Tension was rising on board the American aircraft carrier. The pilots found it hard to prevent signs of their nervousness from becoming apparent. Each of them knew that the moment of truth would soon be upon them. All were extremely eager for action, some with a measure of anxiety; others with an admixture of youthful euphoria. Others, too, had become suddenly silent and uncommunicative as if they were gathering strength for the ordeal; others, on the other hand, gave free rein to their enthusiasm and their aggressive exuberance.

One of them, Lieutenant Powers, who piloted a Dauntless of VS2 and whose outward calm belied his inward exhaltation, boasted that he would not return from the operation without having dropped his bomb on the target. He took an oath that he would sink an enemy aircraft carrier unaided. His fellow pilots regarded his statements as mere bluster and attached no importance to them.

The first certain indication that the decisive confrontation would take place on that day originated from the same piece of good fortune which, on the evening before, had led the Americans to transmit on the same frequency as the one used by the Japanese aircraft. At 0833, one of the *Lexington*'s radio-operators picked up a message from the Japanese reconnaissance plane which had spotted TF17. The message was translated and passed to Fletcher who immediately knew that the enemy must now know with remarkable accuracy his position, the number and type of vessels under his command, his course and his speed. Fletcher's eagerness and anxiety were now doubled, for it needed no great intelligence to grasp the fact that the Japanese were in possession of a great advantage which might well prove catastrophic for the Americans. It was obvious that the enemy, true to form, would not be long in sending over his first strike. In the few minutes which followed, the die would be cast as far as the coming battle was concerned, and Fletcher knew this better than anybody else. The American admiral was like a cat on hot bricks and cursed the misfortune which had enabled the enemy to discover him first.

No more than three minutes could have elapsed between the moment when Fletcher received the translated Japanese message which had been intercepted and the moment when he heard the voice of his first reconnaissance pilot. They were however desperately long minutes. Then, at 0838, contact was made with the enemy by an aircraft piloted by Lieutenant J. G. Smith who reported the position, the composition, the course and the speed of the Japanese striking force. Fletcher boiled with rage when he learnt a little later that Smith had caught sight of the enemy at 0815 but had waited to make certain that his discovery and calculations were accurate before sending his report. This enormous care on his part was not, however, a measure of Smith's accuracy. He had given the position of the Japanese fleet as 12°S, 156°12′E and 175 miles north-east of TF17. All this information proved inaccurate. Lieutenant Commander R. E. Dixon, on board another Dauntless, who was exploring a neighbouring area, changed course and rejoined Smith in order to assist him in maintaining contact. On the strength of the information re-transmitted by TF17, Dixon reached the position reported at about nine o'clock, but without seeing either Smith or the Japanese fleet. Dixon personally undertook a search, but it was not until 0930 that he perceived the Japanese ships heading south at a speed of 25 knots. He took the bearing twice but it was clear that Smith had made a bad mistake. The enemy was in reality 45 miles north of the position given by Smith. This initial error threatened to have very serious consequences. Dixon cleverly took advantage of cloud cover to keep in contact until 1045, at which moment his petrol gauge indicated that he had just enough fuel to regain the *Lexington*.

Knowing that time is a precious and often decisive factor, Fletcher, shortly before 0840, ordered the groups of aircraft which had been ready since dawn to take off. Only then did he hand over the tactical command of operations to Rear-Admiral Fitch, in order to reduce the volume of radio and radar communications and transmissions. On board the carriers, which now buzzed with activity like bee-hives, flight-deck mechanics and pilots were feverishly occupied with the aircraft about to take off. The *Yorktown* sent off 24 Dauntless bombers, nine Devastator torpedo aircraft and six Wildcat fighters, which closed in formation above the aircraft carrier before heading for the enemy at 0915. Ten minutes later, the *Lexington* sent off in her turn 22 Dauntless dive-bombers, 12 Devastators and nine Wildcats, all of which set off on the same course at 0925. A total of 82 American aircraft had been launched against the enemy who in the meantime had 69 aircraft of its own flying along an almost reciprocal course. The two hostile groups of aircraft crossed not long afterwards, but without seeing each other because of masses of cloud.

Fletcher, having just sent off his spearhead and now hoping that fortune would smile on his pilots, sent off an urgent message at ten o'clock, giving his position and also that of the enemy to MacArthur's headquarters, asking for military aircraft to assist in attacking the Japanese ships. As it turned out, MacArthur's aircraft had no hand whatever in the naval battle which was to come and confined themselves to one raid, incidentally fruitless, on the Japanese landing forces as they retreated.

As far as the Japanese were concerned, after its air groups had been launched, the Japanese striking force had adopted a formation which, although not very original, played a very significant part in the battle to come. Rear-Admiral Hara had decided that each of his aircraft carriers should advance separately, escorted by two cruisers and two or three destroyers. It will be remembered that the two heavy cruisers detached from Goto's group had rejoined Takagi the evening before and had thus increased from two to four the strength in heavy cruisers of the striking force. The two separate groups had had orders to sail in line remaining between eight and ten miles apart. This extremely appropriate formation had the aim of making the best use of the intermittent cloud cover which alternated with

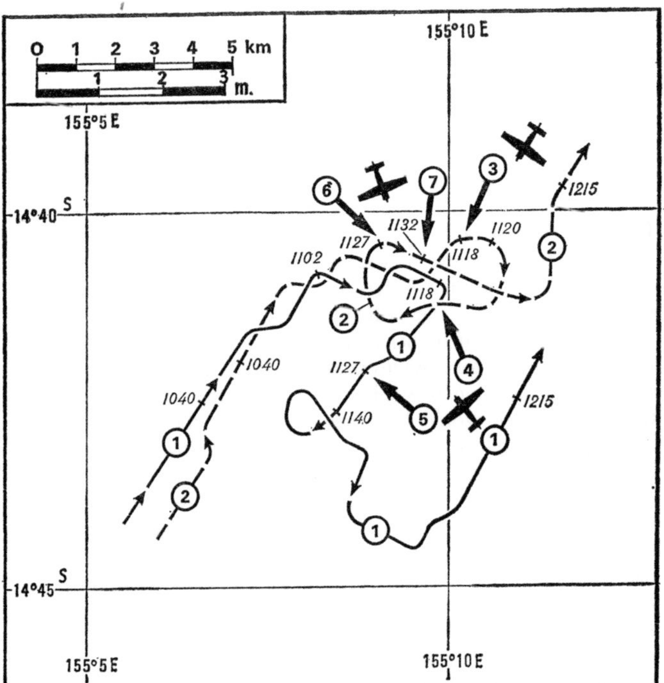

MOVEMENTS OF THE AMERICAN AIRCRAFT CARRIER ON MAY 8 1942

Times given eg. as follows: 1127= 1127 hrs.

1 Course followed by the aircraft carrier *Yorktown* under Japanese attack

2 Course followed by the aircraft carrier *Lexington* under Japanese attack

3 Attack made by *Kate* torpedo aircraft

4 Attack on the *Yorktown* by Japanese torpedo aircraft

5 Attack by *Val* dive-bombers on the *Yorktown*

6 1st attack on the *Lexington* by Japanese dive-bombers

7 2nd attack by *Val* dive-bombers on the *Lexington*

patches of clear sky. These patches were generally of medium size and suggested that if one of the two groups were spotted, the other would be hidden because of the space between them. This is in fact what occurred.

It must be remembered, incidentally, that TF17 was then south of the bad weather area and was consequently in an area of fine weather with a clear and translucent sky in which a few white clouds were gently wafted across an azure background by the fresh trade winds blowing from the south-east.

The American attack

Although the Japanese attacking aircraft had left their aircraft carriers sooner than their American opposite numbers had left theirs, it was the American planes which first made contact with the enemy. This was due to their higher cruising speed and to the fact that they had been ordered, for obvious tactical reasons, to force the pace and make up for lost time. It will be remembered that Fletcher suspected that the Japanese would have taken off from the aircraft carriers before his own pilots. Therefore, to regain the initiative at any price, he had suggested that Admiral Fitch should order his aircraft to increase flying speed. This was possible because the range was relatively short and the aircraft could therefore afford an appreciable increase in their fuel consumption. Moreover, the American aircraft had had rather less distance to travel owing to the direct course and the relative closeness of the two hostile fleets as they sailed towards each other. Lastly, they had the considerable advantage of predominantly south-east winds which helped to speed them on their way towards their objective.

The first aircraft to reach the Japanese fleet were the *Yorktown*'s Dauntless bombers. This happened at about 1030, and the Americans thus regained the slight advantage that they had lost earlier.

Lieutenant Commander Burch, who was heading the Dauntless dive-bombers, had climbed to 1,500 feet and, as arranged, he began a circular holding pattern while waiting for the other air groups. Although no look-out on board the *Zuikaku* had spotted them, the roar of the American engines was clearly audible, and the alarm was sounded on board. The *Shokaku* changed course slightly to come into the wind and launched sufficient *Zero* fighters to reinforce her protective screen.

When, a little before eleven o'clock, all the *Yorktown*'s air groups were assembled, Lieutenant Commander Joe Taylor, head of flight VT5, gave the signal to attack. His nine Devastators peeled off and dived on the *Shokaku* which was the only aircraft carrier visible at that moment. The six Wildcat fighters of flight VF42 followed to protect the slow and vulnerable torpedo-bombers. The Dauntless dive-bombers began their dive soon afterwards.

At this point, the *Zero* single-seater fighters intercepted the Devastators and a dogfight began between the Wildcats and the Japanese fighters. Confused by this interception, which was as resolute as it was abrupt, the American torpedo carriers nevertheless came down very low. They launched their torpedoes from too great a range and these weapons, which were unfortunately but correctly reputed to be excessively slow, bad at depth-keeping and not always certain to explode, all missed their targets.

Two of the Dauntless pilots did however have the satisfaction of dropping two bombs, one after the other, on the *Shokaku*. The first exploded on the starboard side forward of the flight-deck and set fire to an aircraft fuel tank; the second hit the extreme stern and destroyed the aircraft engine repair shop on the lower deck. Both these bombs rendered the *Shokaku* impotent, or to be more exact, put a temporary stop to her air operations. Indeed, the two fires, one forward, the other at the stern, together with the holes caused by the bombs, made any use of the flight-deck impossible. On board the *Zuikaku*, which was at this moment enveloped in a heavy rainstorm, the attack could not be seen, and it was only a few minutes later, when the Japanese flagship emerged from the shower, that Hara discovered that the *Shokaku* was on fire.

It was logical that the work of destruction initiated by the aircraft from the *Yorktown* should be completed and even crowned by the *Lexington*'s air groups. This however did not happen, or rather certain unforeseen events put paid to this hope on the part of the Americans. In the first place, the three Wildcats escorting the 18 Dauntless dive-bombers of flight VB2 lost the planes they were supposed to be protecting in the mass of cloud and, when they failed to find them, turned about and returned to the aircraft carrier. As a result, the Dauntless dive-bombers from flight VB2 wandered for a long time amongst thick cloud without discovering the enemy, although they had steered a course based on excellent data. Their leader, Lieutenant Commander Hamilton, ordered them to make a search, but, seeing nothing and realising that their fuel tanks were half empty,[1] he ordered his pilots to head for TF17. As a result the 18 Dauntless dive-bombers from flight VB2 failed to attack the enemy fleet.

Meanwhile the 12 torpedo aircraft from flight VT2 had also had a great deal of difficulty. A short time after their take-off from the *Lexington*, one of them had mechanical trouble and was obliged to return to the carrier *in extremis*. What was even more serious however, was that the leader, Commander Brett,[2] only knew the enemy's position from Smith's initial report, which meant that he was flying a wrong course. When the 11 Devastators reached the position given by Smith, they found nothing. Brett ordered a search, which was particularly difficult owing to the atmospheric conditions, and they flew round in circles for a long time, using an enormous amount of fuel, and it was not until 1140 that one of them finally located the Japanese fleet.

Meanwhile four Dauntless bombers from flight VS2 and six Wildcat fighters from flight VF2 had joined up and followed the torpedo carriers at a distance, hoping that they would lead them to the target. Their hope was realised and, making use of their speed which was higher than that of the others, Commander Ault, who was leading them, organised an attack. He led his group, together with the 11 Devastators, up to 6,000 feet by artfully making use of the cover provided by the cloud. By doing this he deceived the enemy as to his real intentions, so that they were unable to put up any very effective defence. In the labyrinth of clouds only one Japanese aircraft carrier was to be seen. This was again the *Shokaku*, since the *Zuikaku* was at that moment screened by large and lowering clouds.

The Devastators took advantage of a gap in the clouds to spiral down at high speed to the low altitude required for launching torpedoes. They were followed by the Dauntless dive-bombers, while the Wildcats, which had just caught sight of several Japanese fighters, joined the battle. Very bravely the six American fighters drew their Japanese opposite numbers far enough away from the ships to enable the attacking aircraft to be virtually free from inter-

[1] The aircraft tanks had been filled up overnight and when they took off they were only 88% full. The take-off had been so hurried that there had been no time to complete refuelling operations.

[2] Commander William B. Brett was also the commanding officer of Air Group 2. This meant that he was in charge of all aircraft on board the *Lexington*.

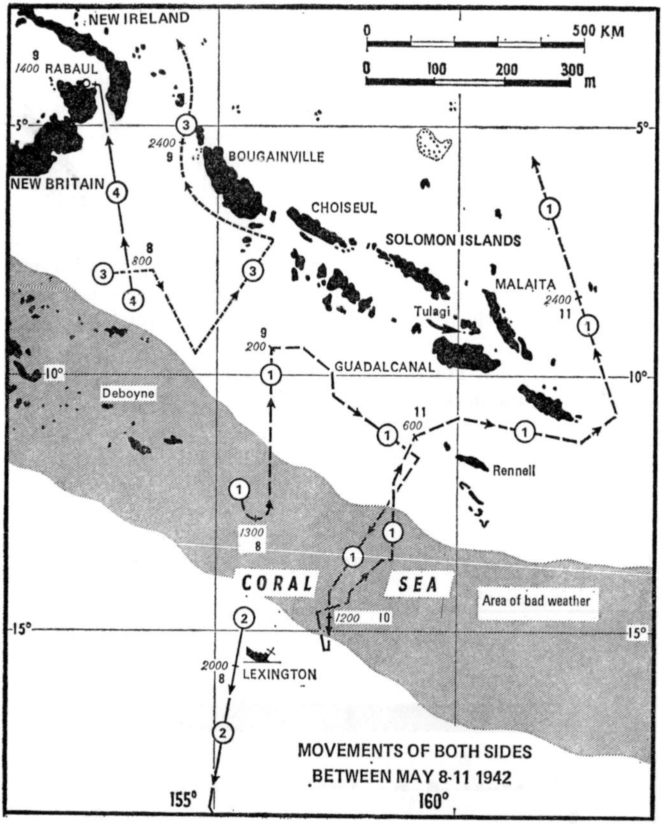

Times given eg. as follows 600= 0600 hrs.

1 Course followed by Japanese striking force reinforced by units from Goto's group
2 Course followed by the retreating Task Force 17
3 Course followed by the retreating Japanese support group on its way to Truk
4 Course followed by the retreating close-support group and the Japanese landing forces retreating to Rabaul

ception. Three of the Wildcats were lost during this diversion. The torpedo aircraft, flying at low speed and almost at surface level, were overtaken by the Dauntless bombers in a high speed dive and all the aircraft attacked more or less at the same time. The Japanese however, who were well aware of the deficiencies of the American torpedoes, had no difficulty in avoiding them, particularly as they had been once again launched from too far away. The Japanese ships were therefore in the act of zig-zagging when the characteristic whistle of the Dauntless dive-bombers was heard.

One of these aircraft, piloted by Lieutenant Powers, did not release its bomb at the usual height of 1,500 feet but pursued its terrifying dive. One of his fellow pilots saw the bomb drop at a height of about 300 feet, which was much too low for the aircraft to escape the blast from the explosion. It was only then that this pilot remembered what Powers had said before setting off. The bomb exploded on the deck of the enemy aircraft carrier while Powers' aircraft was still in the immediate vicinity and had hardly begun to climb away. The Dauntless, caught in the blast of the explosion, rocked, shed part of its wings and stalled into the sea causing the death of a brave pilot and his observer.[1]

Several American aircraft were shot down either by the *Zero* fighters or by Japanese anti-aircraft guns, among them the plane

SHOKAKU

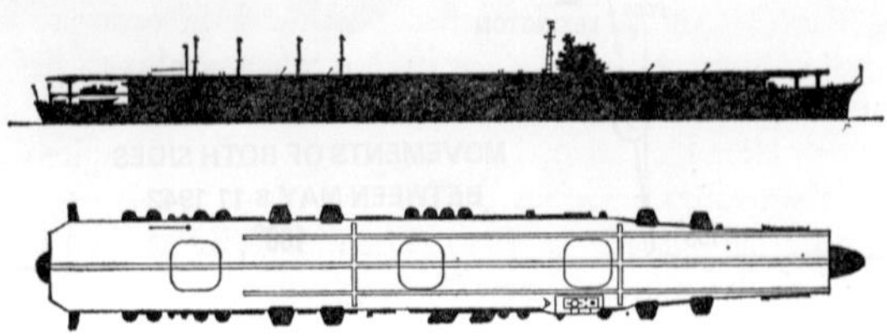

[1] Lieutenant Powers was, as far as is known, the first American pilot to receive the Congressional Medal of Honor, which is the highest distinction awarded by the United States. It is sad to think that this award was posthumous.

piloted by Commander Ault. The *Shokaku* had thus received a total of three 1,000lb bombs and her crew had lost 108 sailors killed, while 40 of her men had been injured. The *Zuikaku* remained unharmed, having been concealed by the clouds throughout the attack.

The remarkable efficiency of the Japanese

As had been feared, the Japanese attack on the American aircraft carriers occurred only a very short time after the American aircraft had attacked the *Shokaku*. Even before the American striking force had had time to take off from the aircraft carriers, senior officers knew that Japanese air attacks were coming. As we have seen, some of them, Fletcher in particular, feared that they might take place before their own aircraft had had time to attack the enemy. This was an indication of the lead the Japanese had gained in spotting the American fleet. Owing to the measures taken by the Americans, their squadrons had made up for lost time and proceeded to attack before the Japanese managed to exploit their advantage. On the basis of the information and evidence available to him, Captain 'Ted' Sherman, the *Lexington*'s commanding officer, had even worked out that the Japanese assault would occur at about eleven o'clock. Captain Sherman also based these calculations on the strength of the enemy transmissions picked up during the morning. (Transmission strength decreases in proportion to range and may thus be used to approximate distance.)

At 1030 Admiral Fitch, who was at that time senior officer in command of air operations, headed north-east in order to reduce the length of the return flight for his aircraft and also to get closer to the enemy. He thus adopted measures that were identical with those which Hara had taken a few moments earlier. Despite Captain Sherman's warning, a serious muddle occurred in the organisation of the fighter aircraft above TF17. The first Wildcats had taken off very early in the morning, and by 1045 most of them were short of fuel and should have landed again to refuel. During the time taken up by these landings and before refuelling could be completed, the American fleet lost a considerable part of its air protection force. The fault lay with the officer in charge of the fighters, who had failed to remember the probable time-table of the enemy attack, which had been stated and restated on several occasions by Captain Sherman. Within the same period, the American look-outs were given instructions to redouble their efforts in order to make up for this mistake, and the extra safety precautions required had fortunately been taken before the enemy arrived. When action stations were sounded, all gun crews were recalled to their posts and all watertight doors were closed. However, because there were still fighters which were in the process of refuelling, the aviation fuel taps were left on. In spite of the serious risk of fire this entailed, it was impossible to do otherwise. At that moment, Admiral Fitch, who was afraid of needlessly losing the 23 Dauntless dive-bombers available, which were to form the second wave of attack, ordered them to take off. This was a very wise action, since it ensured that the aircraft would not be destroyed without a fight should their aircraft carrier be attacked. It also took care of the future, since these aircraft could thus return after the attack and would again be ready for service. The 23 Dauntless aircraft therefore took off complete with fuel and ammunition, but without bombs.

In confirmation of Captain Sherman's calculations, the *Lexington*'s radar detected the enemy at 1055, and the operator announced:

'Large numbers of echoes 70 miles north-east.'

As Admiral Fitch had feared, there were only eight Wildcats above the fleet at this moment, and these were short of fuel and waiting to land. The eight fighter pilots received orders to stay in the air but to remain close to the aircraft carriers.

The two aircraft carriers then changed course south-east, heading into the wind and increased speed to 30 knots in order to launch the nine Wildcats which had been refuelled after landing a few moments before. The first five of these were instructed to keep in front of the enemy. Two others were to remain at low level in order to intercept the Japanese torpedo aircraft which were waiting to attack first, in accordance with the enemy's usual tactics.

Thus, the error made by the officer commanding the fighters meant that the Americans were unexpectedly caught at an extremely unfavourable moment, and the few aircraft they had sent off in the enemy's direction had been given a task which was almost impossible to carry out owing to the overwhelming numerical superiority of the Japanese in regard to fighters. TF17, therefore, was defended by only 17 Wildcat fighters, of which nine belonged to the *Lexington* and were in a fit state to attack the enemy, while the other eight from the *Yorktown* had almost empty fuel tanks. This was a very small force to set against the numerous *Zero* fighters which were already known to outclass the American Wildcats from a technical point of view.

The two Wildcat fighters which had been sent off to intercept the *Kate* torpedo-bombers soon ran into a pack of *Zero* fighters for which they were no match. The three other Wildcats, which had been the last to take off from the *Lexington*, climbed as quickly as possible in order to intercept the Japanese *Val* dive-bombers, but, only a little above 9,000 feet, they could see the enemy aircraft arriving in formation a long way above them. Under these conditions their action lost its element of surprise and also any advantage which they might have gained from a rapid attack.

As for the four Wildcats which had taken off earlier and had also been instructed to intercept the enemy at maximum height, they made a wide circuit, which meant that they could not gain sufficient height. Their leader, realising that under these conditions interception was impossible, gave the order to turn round and fly back over the fleet in order to defend it at close quarters. TF17's air defence was therefore not particularly brilliant. Admiral Fitch however suggested using the 23 Dauntless dive-bombers without bombs as interceptors. It would be impossible to expect them to cope with the formidable Japanese fighters, but their relatively high speed could be effectively used against the enemy's slower heavy torpedo aircraft. This was not the first occasion on which a Douglas Dauntless had been used without its bombs as a substitute for a fighter, but it was the first time that it had been done officially. The pilots of the Dauntless dive-bombers accepted their new rôle willingly although they knew that their chances of success were not good.

From their patrolling height of 1,800 feet, they bravely dived to attack the *Kates* which were approaching, still protected by the *Zeros*. Within a few minutes, four Japanese torpedo aircraft were shot down, but four dive-bombers suffered a similar fate. Despite this courageous action, the senior officers of TF17 were well aware that in the last resort they could really rely only on their ships' anti-aircraft defences to beat off the enemy attack. These defences went into action a little before 1115.

Some minutes earlier, the American look-outs had spotted the enemy approaching from the north-east with the sun behind him. The wind had backed slightly and trade winds were blowing freshly from the east at a speed of 18 knots (20mph). In accordance with custom, the Japanese first sent in their torpedo aircraft, which almost immediately divided into three groups flying at a low level of between 60 and 150 feet. Two of these groups attacked the *Lexington* from both sides at once; the third went for the *Yorktown* but only from one side.

The American gunners tried to put up a wall of fire and steel to ward off their assailants, but most of their shots went wide. Nevertheless, one of the first of the *Kates*, which was on the point of launching its torpedo, received a direct hit from a 127mm shell so that it disintegrated into an enormous ball of fire, in which the aircraft, its torpedo and its reserve fuel tanks all exploded together. For a moment the body of one of the members of the Japanese crew could be seen flying through the air before disappearing into the sea.

One officer, who was on the *Lexington*'s bridge and who had his binoculars trained on the Japanese torpedo aircraft, noticed that they were equipped with a missile of a peculiar shape. He later described the Japanese torpedoes as having what seemed to be wooden boxes round both their warhead and their rear fins. This solved a riddle which had been shrouded in mystery ever since Pearl Harbor. The Japanese ability to launch their torpedoes so quickly and so high was now crystal clear. The wooden boxes absorbed the shock of the torpedoes' impact with the water and kept the missiles from diving too deep. This meant that all the essential organs of the torpedoes remained intact until they exploded.

The *Kates* dropped their 'fish' at a range of some 1,000 yards, after which they broke off to climb away out of range of the American anti-aircraft guns. When the first enemy torpedo dropped to starboard of the *Lexington*, Captain Sherman ordered the quartermaster to put the helm hard down so as to present the aircraft carrier's stern to the torpedoes. He was obliged to cancel this order immediately however, on hearing Commander H. S. Duckworth, who was in charge of the *Lexington*'s aircraft strength, suddenly shout:

> 'Don't change course, Captain! There's a torpedo on each side of us running parallel!'

The great aircraft carrier was not easy to manoeuvre and her minimum turning radius (1,650 yards) was relatively large. Captain Sherman made every effort however to present the smallest possible area of the *Lexington*'s vast hull to the deadly menace of the Japanese torpedoes. The vessel, whose framework groaned under the violent and exaggerated movements of her rudder, managed to avoid 11 enemy torpedoes. This was no mean feat for a ship of 40,000 tons fully laden.

But the number and above all the speed of the Japanese torpedoes were soon too much for Captain Sherman's resourcefulness. At 1120 the first torpedo struck the *Lexington* on the forward port side, followed by another also on the port side below the bridge. The 'Lady Lex' shuddered throughout her length, for she was severely wounded although not mortally.

Although the anti-aircraft defence put up that day by the American ships was far from being what it was later to become, it nevertheless impressed the Japanese pilots, who were also meeting their adversaries for the first time. In this context we cannot do better than quote Captain Shigekazu Shimazaki, leader of the torpedo group on board the *Zuikaku*. Of his attack on the *Lexington* he wrote:

> 'Never had I imagined a fight of this kind! When we attacked the enemy aircraft carriers, we encountered a veritable wall of anti-aircraft fire. The aircraft carriers and their escorts darkened the sky with their tracer bullets, shells and shrapnel. It seemed impossible that we could survive such a stream of anti-aircraft gunfire. Both our *Zeros* and the American Wildcats were diving and wheeling in the very centre of our formations. Aircraft were going down in flames on all sides. During this tempest of fire, I came down almost to water level in order to launch my torpedo at the *Lexington*. I had to fly on the crests of the waves to keep out of this terrific bombardment. In fact I was so low that I almost crashed into the bow of the ship, for I was a long way below the level of her flight deck. I could clearly see the sailors on the *Lexington*, who were staring at my aircraft as if petrified all the time I was approaching. I do not know if I could live through such terrible moments again.'[1]

Meanwhile the third group of Japanese torpedo carriers had launched eight torpedoes at the port bow of the *Yorktown*. Captain Buckmaster was fortunate enough to be attacked only on one side; he also had the advantage of commanding a much more manoeuvrable vessel than the *Lexington*. The radius of her turning circle was 920 yards and the *Yorktown* heeled when turning through 90°, thus managing to evade all the torpedoes launched. According to eye witnesses, one of these torpedoes came within 10 yards of her hull.

At the very moment when the American ships were involved in

[1] Masatake Okumiya, Jiro Horikoshi and Martin Caidin – 'Les Ailes japonaises en guerre', published by Les Presses de la Cité – Paris 1956.

their evasive action with the results described, the Japanese dive-bomber attacks began. These were made from a height of 1,500 feet and encountered virtually no opposition. A few Wildcat fighters which had survived the engagement with the *Zeros* had gone off in pursuit of the Japanese torpedo aircraft and were too far away and too low to be able to intervene. Had they done so, they would have encountered an enemy greatly superior in numbers and protected by numerous *Zero* fighters. The pilots of the *Val* bombers split up between the two main targets presented by the American aircraft carriers, and dived. After a screaming dive lasting about 30 seconds, they dropped their bombs at about 2,400 feet and levelled out at between 1,500 and 1,800 feet before climbing back into a sky dotted with bursting shells and columns of smoke.

The *Lexington* would seem to have had the doubtful privilege of being hit first. At 1125 a light bomb exploded on the port bow in the middle of a stack of 127mm shells. A somewhat heavier bomb also landed on the susperstucture beside the funnel and caused a great deal of damage. Several other bombs fell in the water, three of them so close to the ship's sides that the plates were split or dented in many places. The victims of these bombs included Commander Gilmore, the ship's paymaster, and Commander Trojalkowski, the dental surgeon.

The anti-aircraft gunfire continued, but failed to reach the density required to shake, let alone break up the diving attack of the Japanese. The noise was ear-shattering; gun shots mingled with the thunder of bursting shells, the screaming roar of dive-bombers, the uproar of exploding bombs and the shouts of the sailors. One minor contributor to the general uproar was the prolonged and lugubrious wail of the ship's siren which had been set off by a bomb explosion which severed the control mechanism.

The group of dive-bombers which had converged on the *Yorktown* had also achieved an equally sinister result. At 1120 Captain Buckmaster's vessel was hit by an 800lb bomb which penetrated the flight deck abreast of the island and exploded on the fourth deck, destroying one large compartment, killing 37 men and wounding 33 others. Fire broke out immediately.

The *Yorktown*'s violent manoeuvres undoubtedly confused the Japanese bomb aimers and they failed to score any more hits, although two other bombs fell close alongside, denting the hull, but without causing any vital damage.

At 1140, to everyone's general surprise and whilst all eyes were scanning the sky, a *Kate* torpedo aircraft came down very low and launched its torpedo. Captain Buckmaster, who was immediately informed, boldly ordered a change of course just in time to bring the aircraft carrier parallel to the missile. The menacing torpedo passed more than 150 feet away and disappeared. The last attack also marked the close of the battle. The Japanese bombers had re-grouped in the air above and were already flying northwards. The engagement between the rival naval aircraft had lasted about 20 minutes.

Throughout the battle, the escorting American cruisers and destroyers had had a great deal of difficulty in following the violent and unpredictable movements of the aircraft carriers. They had therefore distributed themselves around each flagship in such a way as to provide gunfire support to the aircraft carriers which were the sole target of the Japanese attack.

On board both the *Lexington* and the *Yorktown*, the officers responsible for the various sections had already begun to tot up their losses, while the damage control and fire fighting squads continued to staunch the jets of incoming water and smother the fires. Only a few minutes after the Japanese aircraft had departed, the *Yorktown*'s fire fighting squad managed to put out her fires, and it was discovered with great satisfaction that the damage to the deck caused by the enemy bomb was close enough to the island not to interfere with air operations. Consequently, soon after the attack, the American aircraft were able to take off and land once again. This mitigated the disastrous effects of losing so many aircraft.

The 'Lady Lex' in trouble

As a result of her injuries, the *Lexington* had a list of 7° to port and three of her boiler rooms were almost full of water; also there were still three fires which had yet to be extinguished. It was typical of the crew and all the other personnel on board that nobody felt discouraged but took a very active part in the struggle to get the ship back to a condition of operational effectiveness. Captain Sherman, assisted by highly efficient officers, inspired his men with so much energy that positive results were soon apparent. In the bowels of the ship, fuel oil was pumped into the wing tanks. This reduced the vessel's list, and a start was made on pumping out the ship. At about 1230 the fires were extinguished and the flight deck again ready for air operations. True, the repairs were only temporary, but the great ship was able to move and could once more operate her aircraft.

With characteristic humour, Commander H. R. 'Pop' Healy, head of the *Lexington*'s damage control section, arrived about 1240 to report to Captain Sherman in words which finished as follows:

> '. . . We have stopped up the holes made by the torpedoes, the fires are now out and the vessel will be almost back on an even keel in a few moments, but, may I suggest, Captain, that if you intend to be hit by any other torpedoes it would be as well to take them on the starboard side!'

The situation was thus a long way from being critical. Although the 'Lady Lex' was wounded, she appeared far from ending her days. Everyone on board considered that a few weeks in port would restore her completely. Some officers even thought that the *Lexington* would be able to put to sea and be fully operational within two months.

It was then that the catastrophe occurred. At 1247 the air was rent by a terrible explosion which made the huge hull quiver from stem to stern. The ship's very frames seemed to crack under the enormous blast.

It took a few minutes to establish the cause of the accident. The aviation fuel supply pipes had been shaken by the repeated explosions of Japanese torpedoes and bombs to such an extent that they had fractured, and the volatile gases had spread throughout the lower parts of the ship without warning, through doorways to compartments and the fore and aft gangways. Eventually, the gases had accumulated in an electrical generator compartment which was operating. A spark did the rest. Fire broke out again at several points and one internal explosion followed another. The telephone wires were cut in various compartments, considerably impeding the work of damage control teams, who were not only cut off but were unable to get at the places worst affected, which of course were the ones it was essential to restore to service. One of the explosions occurred in a command post and claimed a very large number of victims, among them Commander Healy, who was seriously injured. After that, any attempt to co-ordinate the remaining salvage operations became extremely difficult if not impossible. Soon the sky was red and black with flames and a thick column of smoke emerging from within the ship.

Despite this fatal blow, the air operations which had begun before the explosion were continued for a few more minutes. At 1345 however, it was necessary to call them off owing to the deep black cloud which rendered the flight deck almost invisible and to the threat of explosion which was now continuous. Despite the great danger, a few aircraft returned from their attack on the Japanese ships and nevertheless managed to land.

The *Lexington* was still steaming at 25 knots however, and the mere fact that she could still keep up this speed and provide the electrical energy which was essential for the damage control and fire fighting squads to operate, still gave some cause for hope. The second-in-command, Commander Mort Seligman, gave himself whole-heartedly to the task of encouraging the men who were so bravely struggling to stop up these fresh leaks in the hull and to extinguish the fires at source. The fires unfortunately were not receding; indeed in some places they were gaining. By 1430, conditions were so bad that Captain Sherman was informed that the fires could no longer be fought in some of the ship's compartments. The damage control and fire fighting squads therefore withdrew after closing the water-tight doors. From now on things were to get worse.

At 1445 another violent explosion destroyed the boiler-room ventilation system. This immediately forced up the temperature in the compartments and the heat was soon too great for men to be able to stay at their posts. Choking, they quitted the boiler rooms, and the ship's speed was quickly reduced. 'The "Lady Lex" was really very sick!', one survivor said later. At about 1515 it was necessary to suspend all air movements, which had been partially resumed a short time previously. The last American aircraft from the raid on the enemy fleet, together with those that had covered TF17, were directed on to the *Yorktown*, which recovered 19 of them.

A few moments before, at 1510, Admiral Fletcher had resumed command of Task Force 17 and he now sent the destroyer *Morris* to the *Lexington*'s aid. The destroyer, at considerable risk to herself, went alongside the aircraft carrier and her largest fire hoses were manned. The extent of the damage was so great however, that they were of no avail. Captain Sherman later said that the fires had reached such a pitch that it was impossible to fight them. Fresh explosions continually occurred on the lower decks, causing even greater damage and claiming an ever increasing number of victims.

General Douglas MacArthur (62 years old in 1942) whose forces, based in Australia, tried to support Fletcher's forces, but took no active part in the battle itself. It was MacArthur's aircraft however which were the first to report Japanese movements in the Solomon Islands.

NEW ZEALAND
WELLINGTON
AUCKLAND
TASMAN SEA
Tasmania
Bass Str.
MELBOURN
ADELAIDE
CANBERRA
SYDNY
NEWCASTLE
BRISBANE
AUSTRALIA
PERTH
INDIAN OCEAN
PORT HEDLAND
BROOME
DERBY
TOWNSVILLE
CORAL SEA
Timor Sea
PORT DARWIN
MILNE B.
HORN I.
Torres Str.
Arafura Sea
KUPANG
Sunda Is
TIMOR
Solomon Is
P. MORESBY
MERAUKE
SALAMAUA
LAE
TENINBER Is
SURABAYA
ARU Is
RABAUL
New Guinea
MACASSAR
N

Left: This map, from an English-language propaganda news sheet circulated by the Japanese at the end of April 1942, shows Australia, the southern part of New Guinea and the attacks planned by the Japanese forces. Some of the aims illustrated were realised, but some were made abortive as a direct result of the battle of the Coral Sea.

Above: On the island of Shortland the Japanese had set up a large reconnaissance seaplane base from which these large 4-engine Kawanishi 97 H6K4's (*Mavis*) followed the course set by the American fleet.

Below: The SBD3 Douglas Dauntless was responsible for the hits recorded on the Japanese aircraft carriers *Shoho* and *Shokaku*.

Top: The Japanese dive-bomber Aichi 99 D3A2 (*Val*), although old in design, was one of the most effective destroyers of American ships.

Above: The famous single-seater fighter Mitsubishi A6M2 Zero (*Zeke*) effectively fought off attacks by American carrier aircraft.

Top: The standard bomber/torpedo aircraft Nakajima 97 B5N2 (*Kate*) scored numerous successes, particularly in torpedo launching formations.

Above: TBD 1 Douglas Devastators failed to achieve the standard expected of them, many being unable to attack, forced down or else driven off by Japanese *Zero* fighters.

Above: In the hands of experienced pilots such as 'Butch' O'Hare, the Grumman F4F 3 Wildcat recorded several victories despite its inferiority from every point of view except that of protection against direct hits.

Below: Admiral Chester W. Nimitz, Head of the Pacific Fleet (CINCPAC), and 'Bull' Halsey, commander of the South-West Pacific theatre, were delighted at the outcome of the battle of the Coral Sea.

Right: The abandonment of the aircraft carrier USS *Lexington* was carried out in an atmosphere of the utmost calm. On her starboard side can be seen the destroyer USS *Morris* (DD417) endeavouring to control the fires which unfortunately proved the great aircraft carrier's undoing.

Above: The fate of the USS *Lexington* was finally sealed by the explosion of petrol fumes which had built up in various compartments and which aggravated the damage she had already sustained.

Below: The aircraft carrier USS *Enterprise* seen from ¾ aft. Together with USS *Hornet*, she arrived too late to take part in the battle, but her approach helped to scare off the Japanese.

Shortly afterwards, an officer reported that the torpedo warheads in the hangars on the lower deck had reached the critical temperature of 60°C and were liable to explode spontaneously. The fire was gaining ground and was approaching the bomb magazine, thus threatening to blow up the entire vessel. Captain Sherman had already given orders to evacuate the wounded, the sick and those who had been poisoned by the burning gases, and they had been put into the lifeboats. He had also ordered off the aircraft pilots, who were now of no use, and these had been taken on board the destroyer *Morris* which was still alongside.

Meanwhile, the heat had risen to such intensity in the engine rooms, that it was completely impossible to remain in them. All personnel had been given the order to open all valves as they left, to shut off the ventilation supply and to take to the upper decks. Finally, at 1630 the *Lexington* ceased to move.

Orders were given to prepare to abandon ship, a procedure which had not yet commenced. Doctors, sick bay attendants, officers and volunteers showed outstanding bravery by risking their lives to go back down into the ship in order to rescue anyone who might still be below decks. These men, by exploring the entire length of the vessel and by entering compartments in which the heat was unbearable, succeeded in saving 150 more wounded whom they brought back on deck and placed in the lifeboats.

It was then clear that nothing more could be done to save the 'Lady Lex'. In view of the futility of all the efforts which had been made to save the aircraft carrier, Admiral Fitch decided to leave the ship a little before 1700, but he could not bring himself to do so before urging Captain Sherman to follow his example. Sherman hesitated for several apparently interminable minutes before making up his mind to abandon the vessel for which he had so much affection, and it was not until 1707 that the wisdom of the admiral's advice prevailed and Sherman reluctantly decided to give the general order to abandon ship.[1]

As we saw at the beginning of this account, all on board the *Lexington* had an affection for the vessel which very few ships have enjoyed, and it was with sadness that they prepared to abandon her. Meticulously, they got ready the rafts and the last remaining life-

[1] It must be remembered that on board ship the captain is the one and only man in command and takes orders from nobody as to the safe conduct of his vessel.

boats, while a few of them unrolled the safety nets and ropes along the vessel. As a matter of routine, which was rigidly adhered to, the sailors took off their shoes, lined them up on the flight deck and awaited their turn to leave the vessel, well disciplined and in impeccable order. Never had a ship been abandoned with so much phlegmatic calm. There was no evidence of fear or panic.

This atmosphere may be illustrated by the behaviour of a group of men whom Sherman, while making a tour of inspection on the flight deck, found near the port anti-aircraft catwalk waiting patiently 'just as if they were at a bus stop', as a witness was later to say. When he approached them and was about to utter some words of encouragement, he was greeted by these sailors, led by Marine Sergeant Peyton, who gave three hearty cheers in his honour. Sherman was so touched that he could find no words with which to reply.

Rear-Admiral Kinkaid directed salvage operations, while the cruisers *Minneapolis* and *New Orleans* together with the destroyers *Anderson* and *Hammann*, plus the *Morris*, came close in to pick up the sailors who were swimming in water which was fortunately calm and warm. None of these men, nor indeed any of those who had left the ship on rafts or in lifeboats was lost, thanks to the calm weather and everybody's patience. It was a perfect example of how to abandon ship, even perhaps unprecedented in naval history. The extraordinary discipline which reigned during the abandonment of the *Lexington* was so complete that one could see the sailors, who were waiting to go over the side, turn back to the men distributing ice-cream in order to take extra helpings with them. Even Captain Sherman's dog was saved.

The crew of the *New Orleans*[1] took a particular interest in the men rescued from the *Lexington*, and the ship's chaplain, Lieutenant Commander Howell M. Forgy, was indefatigable in the care and attention he devoted to large numbers of wounded.

To satisfy their own consciences Captain Sherman and Commander M. T. Seligman, the second-in-command, assessed the amount of time left to the unfortunate *Lexington* and carried out a final inspection. They visited a large number of compartments which were still accessible and assured themselves that no living person was left on board. While they were making this inspection, another explosion

[1] The 'NO Boat' was the nickname given to this cruiser by the American sailors.

occurred quite close to them in the ship and they reappeared on deck with their uniforms covered in debris and live sparks.

This last great explosion, which occurred at 1830, came from the torpedo store, in which between 14,000 and 18,000lb of warheads had just blown up. This extremely powerful explosion made a hole in the flight deck near the central lift and threw an enormous amount of debris high into the air.

In accordance with tradition, the *Lexington*'s two senior officers were last to leave, and, when all the men had been picked up, Admiral Fletcher gave the destroyer *Phelps* instructions to put an end to her suffering. At eight o'clock four torpedoes were launched, but it seems that only one hit the aircraft carrier. The 'Lady Lex' then gave the impression of being alive; she quivered under the shock as if shuddering with grief. She remained afloat for some time yet, then, with one last heave, sank slowly beneath the sea. She disappeared, bow first, in position 15°12′S and 155°27′E, taking with her the bodies of 216 members of her crew and the remains of 36 aircraft.

Thanks to the exemplary behaviour of the men evacuating the vessel, 2,735 officers and ratings were saved, ie. the *Lexington*'s entire crew with the exception of those killed during the battle or by the subsequent explosions, Even under these conditions, the *Lexington*'s loss was deeply felt in the United States, and appreciably modified the temporary balance sheet which had been drawn up at the moment when the Japanese aircraft regained their aircraft carrier. Actually, the Americans were at that moment claiming the probable destruction of the *Shoho*, one of the two large Japanese tactical aircraft carriers, and a significant amount of damage to the other, whereas the *Yorktown* and the *Lexington* seemed at that time only to be moderately damaged. The balance sheet thus indicated an indisputable tactical victory. In this too, pilots' reports had been too optimistic, since one Japanese aircraft carrier, the *Zuikaku*, remained intact, while the other, the *Shokaku*, had been severely enough hit to have to spend several months in a Japanese dockyard, but her days were in no way numbered.

The attack on the *Yorktown* and the *Lexington* had cost the Japanese 30 aircraft, including Takahashi's, plus 13 others lost as a result of accidents or during landing. The Americans had suffered the loss of 33 aircraft in combat or for other reasons. In other words, the United States Navy had virtually lost the air strength of the *Lexington*, including 36 aircraft which had gone down with the aircraft carrier, while the *Yorktown* still had a considerable air potential, thanks to the 19 aircraft saved from the *Lexington*.

On the Japanese side, the pilots' exaggerations were at least as optimistic, if not more so, since, during their return flight, the Japanese pilots announced that they had sunk a large aircraft carrier of the *Saratoga* class and set fire to another of the *Enterprise* class. On landing on the *Zuikaku*, the Japanese pilots gave so many details that Takagi's staff officers assumed that their results were indeed as they described, and sent a message to this effect to Admiral Yamamoto. The latter, who was furious at Inoue's decision to cancel the landing at Port Moresby, was consoled by this comforting news.

When the *Lexington* fulfilled the Japanese pilots' expectations by sinking, the initial balance was completely upset, since against the loss of one large American aircraft carrier, the Japanese had lost only the far less important *Shoho*. Despite rather larger losses in aircraft, the Japanese naval losses were much less serious, particularly in terms of tonnage. It might therefore seem at first sight as if the battle of the Coral Sea was a tactical victory for the Japanese, if only because the Imperial Fleet had inflicted greater losses on the enemy than it suffered itself.

Nevertheless, a more detailed study of this battle in relation to the aims and achievements of Operation *MO* shows that the Japanese had been precipitate in abandoning the landing at Port Moresby, on which the entire operation was based. From this point of view, the loss of the *Lexington* can be seen as an acceptable price to pay for what later proved to be a great strategic victory for the Americans, although at that time the Allies did not yet know that the threat to Port Moresby and therefore to Australia had not only been averted, but permanently ruled out. Never again were the Japanese to risk a sortie in this region.

American epilogue

Admiral Nimitz at Pearl Harbor had been kept informed of the battle at every stage, and, when he heard the initial results of the Japanese air attack, he sent a signal to Fletcher ordering him to withdraw. This order coincided with Fletcher's own feelings, and, on the night of May 8–9, when the task of rescuing the crew of the *Lexington* had been completed, Fletcher instructed TF17 to head south.

At dawn on May 9, Fletcher's ships altered course to the eastward, just as Nimitz, for one brief moment, had the idea of ordering them to reverse course, thinking that it might still be possible to destroy a few more Japanese vessels. This idea was quickly discarded, however, and the original orders confirmed, because of the objection raised by Nimitz's staff, viz. that it was unreasonable to risk the only aircraft carrier available in the area, particularly as it would be needed in the impending action off Midway. Moreover, since the Japanese aims had been thwarted, it was not strictly necessary to begin a fresh engagement, the outcome of which was by no means certain.

Although the battle was over, there was still a certain element of tenseness in the atmosphere, and Fletcher was careful to keep a good look-out astern. As from dawn on May 9 he flew off various reconnaissance aircraft so as to make sure that the Japanese were not following. During the morning, one of his aircraft reported an enemy aircraft carrier 175 miles north-west. As usual, Fletcher informed MacArthur, at the same time flying off dive-bombers to attack the target indicated.

Contrary to all expectations and for the first time since the start of the operation, MacArthur's staff also sent out 14 military bombers. They approached the spot indicated and found that what the reconnaissance patrol had thought to be an aircraft carrier was a minute island projecting from the ocean. The observer had mistaken the white foam of breakers for the wake of a ship. The effect of this incident was to intensify the bad relations already existing between American military and naval pilots.

However, MacArthur's pilots did not dwell on their disappointment and other sorties were made, particularly against the Japanese seaplane base on Deboyne Island. The Americans wiped out both aircraft and base so thoroughly that the Japanese were forced to abandon the island never to return.

Final Japanese reactions

We should meanwhile examine the effects on the Japanese side of the American air attack. Following this attack, the Japanese aircraft carrier *Shokaku* had, as we know, been seriously damaged. Accordingly, when her commanding officer asked for permission to return to base, Takagi made no objection, believing that the enemy, or at least a considerable part of his effective forces in the area, had been destroyed. The *Shokaku* was not in danger of being lost, but she was incapable of operating her aircraft. Indeed most of them, like those which had returned from attacking the Americans, had landed on the *Zuikaku*. At 1300 therefore, the *Shokaku* received permission to proceed separately to Japan.

The carrier's plating, although not pierced below the water-line, had been displaced in some areas by the blast from near misses. No notice had been taken of this, and, during her homeward voyage, the *Shokaku* nearly sank. It was therefore in a serious condition that she reached Japan, and repairs took more than two months.

Although, for Admiral Inoue, Operation *MO* had been a set-back, he was overjoyed at having destroyed 'two' American carriers and in view of this success, he instructed Takagi at 1800 on May 8 to return to his base at Truk. In order to reassure Admiral Yamamoto, Inoue postponed the landing at Port Moresby to July 3, when the ships about to take part in the action off Midway would once more be available.

Opinions vary widely on the strange attitude adopted by the Commander of Operation *MO*, but one question in particular springs to mind: why did Inoue not follow up the Americans' 'loss' of two large aircraft carriers to land his invasion force which at that time would have encountered very little resistance? Admiral Crace's Task Force 44 was far to the south at the time, and there was no Allied ship of any kind in the Jomard Passage, or indeed anywhere near it. The opportunity was there for the taking, but Inoue insisted on withdrawing. It may well be that he feared attacks from MacArthur's aircraft, particularly as he no longer had the support either of the *Shoho*, which had been sunk, or of Takagi's forces, whose air losses had been considerable and whom he himself had instructed to withdraw.

This over-cautiousness has remained a mystery, since it was certainly not typical of the Japanese, especially at a moment when the fortunes of war were in their favour, and especially since Admiral Yamamoto was against excessive caution and took far more energetic measures when he learned of the situation and the state of his ships. Suspecting that the pilots' reports had greatly exaggerated the actual destruction caused, at midnight on May 8, he ordered Takagi to turn round and sail southward in order to destroy what remained of the American naval forces.

At two o'clock in the morning of May 9, the striking force therefore reversed course and headed at first south-east but a little later south-west in search of the Americans. Takagi carried out his orders to the letter, but he was convinced that the enemy had far too great a start to be overtaken.

In accordance with identical instructions from Yamamoto's HQ, Admiral Goto's covering force rejoined Takagi at noon on May 10 and both continued the search until 1300 on the same day. Persuaded that pursuit would be fruitless, Takagi decided to give up the search and steer northwards. On the following day, May 11, Yamamoto confirmed his order for a general withdrawal.

On May 10, however, in accordance with the conditions specified in Operation *MO*, Admiral Shima's naval force left Rabaul with the aim of occupying the islands of Nauru and Ocean. On May 11, in the middle of the Solomon Islands, the American submarine S.42 caught sight of Shima's fleet, closed in on it and torpedoed the supply vessel *Okinoshima*, which was also the flagship of the force. On hearing of this loss, Admiral Inoue suspended operations until such time as the American submarines operating in the area had returned to their bases.

The landing on the two islands concerned would doubtless have been carried out during the days that followed but for the fact that on May 15 a Japanese reconnaissance aircraft from the air base on Tulagi spotted American aircraft carriers 450 miles east of the Solomons. These were the carriers *Enterprise* and *Hornet* which Nimitz had belatedly and at great risk despatched in the hope that they would be able to support Fletcher. In face of this new and very serious danger, Inoue cancelled the operation he planned and, on the same day, ordered the landing force to fall back on Truk.[1]

This concluded both the battle of the Coral Sea and the operations associated with it. The two aircraft carriers *Enterprise* and *Hornet* were urgently recalled to Pearl Harbor in order to take part in the battle which was impending in the waters off Midway.

TF17 split up into two groups in the afternoon of May 11. Admiral Kinkaid and Rear-Admiral Smith's cruisers steered a course for Noumea, while Fletcher took the *Yorktown* and her escort to Tongatabu to refuel. From there the *Yorktown* went on to Pearl Harbor as quickly as possible, and, thanks to repairs which were carried out with the utmost despatch, she was able to take part in the coming great air and naval confrontation off Midway.

[1] The islands of Nauru and Ocean were invaded without opposition on August 25 and 26, 1942, and held by the Japanese until the end of the war.

The voyage of the *Neosho*

It will be remembered that the first large Japanese air attack was made on May 7 on one of the two replenishment groups of TF17. The destroyer *Sims* had gone down almost immediately, but the tanker *Neosho*, although crippled, underwent a long and difficult odyssey. Buoyed up by the air in her empty tanks, she continued to float even though part of her crew had abandoned her prematurely and in panic following the Japanese attack.

The hundred or so left on board fought strenuously to put back some life into their vessel. They not only managed to put out the fires on board within a very short time, but also to stop up most of the leaks. The *Neosho*, however, still refused to answer to her rudder, and, from May 7 to 11, drifted west-north-west at the mercy of the trade winds and currents. The PBY Catalina seaplanes based on Noumea made a large number of reconnaissance sorties in search of the tanker, but without success owing to the error made in transmitting her distress signals and the long way she had drifted since then.

On May 9, Admiral Leary, as a last resort, ordered the destroyer *Henley* to find the *Neosho* at all costs. The destroyer set out for the wrongly transmitted position and, of course, failed to find the tanker. The *Henley*'s captain searched vainly over ever-increasing circles, but it was not until noon on May 11 that a Catalina seaplane on patrol finally chanced to catch sight of the *Neosho* a long way from the initial position signalled.

On being informed of this, the *Henley* steamed at full speed until she contacted the *Neosho* in the afternoon of the same day. The *Henley* took off the 123 men left on board and sank 'the great old lady', by torpedoing her. The *Henley* then searched for those of the tanker's crew who had so abruptly abandoned her on May 7, but without success. In the evening of May 12, the *Henley* gave up the search and headed for Brisbane.

On arrival there, Captain Phillips, who commanded the *Neosho*, re-calculated the position of the tanker at the moment when the Japanese attacked, and passed on his new calculations to the destroyer *Helm*, which took up the search. On May 14 she discovered one of the *Neosho*'s rafts, to which were clinging four almost completely exhausted men suffering from both thirst and hunger – the sole survivors out of 68 who had occupied four rafts. These four survivors had spent seven days and nights on their relatively frail and uncomfortable craft. After their dramatic rescue, new regulations and more rigid instructions were drawn up in order to prevent further tragic happenings of this kind.

The first echoes

Although in the introduction to this book we stressed that the ultimate significance of the battle of the Coral Sea was greater than generally believed, the reader will be able to assess its importance for himself from the numerous commentaries which appeared as soon as the facts were known. One must not of course give way either to the enthusiasm or the depression which are often the immediate result of an action. It is necessary to wait until the facts, events and lessons to be learned from it have emerged from the cloud of subjectivity which at first enshrouds them. It is not a bad thing however to quote a few of the immediate reactions to this battle in order to reproduce the climate of the period, which is difficult for a historian to evoke without prejudicing the value and the objectivity of his analysis. We are therefore not drawing any forgone conclusions, but rather assessing the battle's significance within its own historical context and in relation to the situation as a whole. The following quotation will suffice to illustrate the spirit of the time:

> *Press communiqué issued in Washington, Saturday, May 9, 1942*
> 'For the first time since hostilities began in the Far East, the Allied fleet has given battle in the Coral Sea and brought off a brilliant victory against the Japanese invasion forces.'

The *New York Times* did not hesitate to print the following in bold type:

> 'The Japanese have been beaten back after a long battle in the Pacific, in which between 17 and 22 of their ships were either sunk or damaged. The enemy is in flight, pursued by the Allied forces.'

That famous press commentator, Hanson Baldwin, even dared to claim:

> 'that the course of the war both in the Pacific and the World as a whole may well have been entirely changed. . . . This battle bids fair to being one of the greatest in the history of the United States Navy.'

For their part, the Japanese announced that they had destroyed two aircraft carriers and two warships and that they had won a great victory. Some of their commentators went so far as to state that the battle more or less marked the final blow to America's hopes.

On the strength of their reports, Hitler sent a warm telegram of congratulations to his courageous Allies on the other side of the world, which he concluded with one of his customary prophecies:

> 'After this fresh defeat, the warships of the American Navy will hardly dare to oppose the Imperial Navy, since any vessels with presumption enough to join battle with the Japanese Fleet may be regarded as already lost.'

In face of all these comments, which were as absurd as they were untruthful, the Department of State for the United States Navy made the following deliberately laconic statement:

> 'No credence should be given to any claims which have been or will be made by Tokyo regarding this battle.'

For the sake of military secrecy and in order to keep the enemy in the dark as to the real truth or the plans (for the Midway operation of course) then being prepared, the detailed results of the battle of the Coral Sea were not published until a month later, just after the battle of Midway. This deliberate silence did nothing of course to cool down the overheated imaginations of the Americans, some of whom regarded it as evidence of a serious defeat. Subsequent events were to prove, however, that official discretion was both wise and expedient, and the appearance of the *Yorktown* at Midway came as a highly unpleasant surprise to the Japanese.

The great threat to Australia, which was implicit in the Japanese Operation *MO*, assumed so immediate and dramatic an aspect that, a few days earlier, the Australian Premier, Mr. John Curtin, issued the following deeply felt cry of alarm:

> 'The invasion of Australia is a threat which may at any moment become a reality.'

As soon as he was informed of the course the battle was taking, Mr. Curtin did not wait for the outcome to be decided, but addressed the members of the Australian Cabinet in the following words, which have since become famous:

'Today, men are fighting for Australia; no man has any excuse for not fighting unless he is contributing to Australia's war effort.'

To judge from the official communiqués and the comments made either immediately after or within a few days of the engagement, the battle of the Coral Sea was not merely an episode, but an event of great significance, if not a turning-point, in the war.

A modest balance sheet with important consequences

In the light of the facts, it would seem that the battle of the Coral Sea was a tactical gain for the Japanese, but a strategic victory for the Americans. Certain commentators in the United States and elsewhere defined it as a Pyrrhic victory, since the losses were greater on the American than on the Japanese side. This is to some extent true, but, considering what was at stake and, above all, the aims of the Imperial Fleet, the loss of the *Lexington* was a fair price to pay for the strategic results of the battle. It cannot be over-stressed that this battle called so abrupt a halt to Japanese expansion towards the south that Japanese forces never returned to that area. It was the first time since the war had started in the Pacific that the Allies were able to put up any real resistance to the invader and prevent him from achieving any more conquests. The psychological effect of this alone was sufficient to offset the loss of the *Lexington*. Not only was Australia safe (and John Curtin expressed his deep gratitude to the Allied forces which had achieved this success), but the outcome of the battle restored America's morale and readiness to fight.

It is also true that, although the battles which were to be fought during the last two years of the war proved far more profitable from the American point of view and although the Allied losses were considerably less than those incurred by the Japanese, in the spring of 1942 no one could afford to be over-critical in view of the disastrous list of defeats in all theatres.

The Japanese of course announced that they had won a resounding victory, claiming that the Americans were virtually on their knees and that their ultimate defeat was no more than a matter of weeks off owing to the enormous losses they had sustained in the Coral Sea. Tokyo was careful not to state that Operation *MO* had been postponed, that one of the large aircraft carriers would be out of action for several months, that the smaller aircraft carrier *Shoho* had been sunk or that a large number of naval air-pilots had been killed during the engagement. The strategic consequences of the setback thus suffered by the Imperial forces did not achieve the prominence they would have been given at any other time. This was because, (a) the Japanese were still celebrating their extraordinary successes during the initial months of the year, and (b) their Navy was concentrating its attention on the impending battle of Midway, so that the Japanese Naval Command had no time to dwell on the action which had just been played out in the south.

It is probable that if the Midway operation had not been in preparation, the Japanese General Staff would have studied far more closely the action which had just occurred in the Coral Sea. Punitive measures would have been taken and lessons would have been drawn from the reverse they had suffered, particularly as these were their first significant losses in ships and aircraft.[1]

Lessons to be learnt

This battle of the Coral Sea might be given many names. For instance, depending on the episodes which went to make it up, it could be called 'the battle of errors', 'the battle of lost opportunities' or perhaps 'the battle of the blind'. Indeed, both sides made mistakes and took up dispositions which were astonishingly similar. While the Japanese concentrated their carrier aircraft on the tanker *Neosho* and the destroyer *Sims* on May 7 in the mistaken belief that they were dealing with the bulk of the American fleet, Task Force 17 flew off the major part of its air squadrons against the insignificant ships of Admiral Marushige's force. It was entirely by chance that the American pilots discovered Admiral Goto's force and that their action was devoid of results since it ended in the destruction of the aircraft carrier *Shoho*.

After this both sides considered, calculated and discarded the suggestion of launching an attack with surface vessels during the night of May 7/8. Had this operation taken place, it is probable that it would have ended in a Japanese victory owing to the greater experience and formidable efficiency which the Japanese Navy possessed in this type of action. Finally, both fleets were often in complete ignorance of each other's position and were sometimes so close that a direct battle could have been fought. But this did not

[1] See Appendix 3 for Table comparing the naval air losses on both sides during the various engagements which went to make up the battle of the Coral Sea.

occur. The fact that the Americans had radar gave them only a very relative and limited tactical advantage in the ability to detect aircraft at short range.

In the field of air operations, the Japanese were better off than their adversaries, since their reconnaissance aircraft were not only more active but more efficient and discovered the Americans first. Moreover, the Japanese carrier aircraft carried out a more rational plan and achieved a result which was tactically far superior to the Americans'. On the other hand, Japanese land-based aircraft, although covered with laurels and representing the mainstay of Imperial Japanese hopes, played a very disappointing and very ineffective rôle.

In the American camp, the reconnaissance missions carried out by MacArthur's military aircraft did not come up to expectations and, as for the American carrier aircraft, these eloquently revealed their ineffectiveness during the raid on Tulagi and when attacking Takagi's fleet. As we have seen, few aircraft managed to reach their targets and those which did attack produced only very poor results in relation to the risks which they took on this occasion. In particular, the American torpedoes proved to be too slow, often following erratic courses and carrying charges which were frequently ineffective, so that the Japanese had no difficulty in avoiding them.

On the technical plane, the American aircraft again demonstrated their inferiority, quite apart from the poor training and inefficiency of their air crews.[1] To use a rather unorthodox simile, the aircraft carriers might be said to represent long-range guns and the aircraft the shells propelled by them. Unfortunately, the American aircraft proved in many cases to be not shells but damp squibs which consequently often hung fire. We must apologise for both the simile and the severity of judgement contained in it, but it is very clear that the Japanese tactical results were far superior to those of the Americans for a virtually identical number of striking aircraft. The Americans, meanwhile, were perfectly aware of this and did their best to remedy their weaknesses. The outcome of later naval air battles showed that the disappointing American results recorded in the battle of the Coral Sea were not recurring.

From the human point of view, this battle suggests a number of conclusions and reflections as to the participants, who were fighting in accordance with their experience, orders and training and were in no way to blame. We can only regret that the American pilots

[1] Cf. The brief study comparing the aircraft of both sides in Chapter 4.

showed themselves less trained for war than their Japanese counterparts.

In the matter of command however, there is more to be said, for the two methods of organising the forces in question were very different. The two senior officers in command of Operation *MO*, viz. Yamamoto and Inoue, had their headquarters at Truk and Rabaul respectively. Both were too far away from the scene to get a proper picture of events from the messages and reports sent to them. The two commanders were thus forced to make decisions in a very different mental atmosphere from that surrounding the combatants. This would explain the astonishing orders which they issued. In the calm conditions surrounding them, these two naval chiefs could only act according to their temperament, since they had but a distorted view of the real facts. Thus, Yamamoto, for instance, the impetuous and aggressive gambler, gave senseless instructions to pursue the Americans and was ignorant of the arrangements made by Inoue, who was more directly responsible for Operation *MO*. The latter, who was serious-minded, vacillating and easily influenced, dared not continue Operation *MO* once he ceased to be certain of the outcome, and, obsessed as he was with the idea of a possible failure which might well cause him to lose face, and accustomed to the easy victories of the first few months of the war, was strangely overcome with fear when he heard, on the one hand, that Crace's force was south of the Jomard Passage and, on the other, that the *Shoho* was lost. Both factors caused him to act and command in ways which his subordinates could not be said always to understand. They obeyed him blindly, but without necessarily realising the reasons for his instructions. These facts, which must be taken into account in assessing the battle and its outcome, illustrate the principle of Japanese administration, which allowed no initiative to its less senior commanders.

On the other hand, the American command organisation was much more flexible and enabled responsibilities and decisions to be delegated to the man on the spot. While Admiral Nimitz, from Pearl Harbor, carefully watched the developments of the various operations, he only intervened in an advisory capacity. It was Fletcher who exercised command of the forces engaged. This principle of course had the disadvantage of allowing full rein to the impulses and inspiration of the man responsible, which meant that mistakes were likely to occur. Fletcher committed errors, of course, but they were limited in extent and sometimes could be corrected immediately simply because he was on the spot and could make prompt use of the verifiable data available.

For instance, Fletcher's decision to attack Tulagi was an error, the main consequence of which was to give the Japanese an early warning of the presence of at least one American aircraft carrier in the Coral Sea, quite apart from the considerable waste of bombs to gain an insignificant tactical advantage. On the other hand, the decision made by Fletcher, who was the only man in a position to make it, to split up his forces and instruct Admiral Crace to block the Jomard Passage, was a stroke of genius which not only decided the strategic outcome of the battle, but which also gave the death blow to Japanese military expansion towards the south.

We said earlier that the American pilots had not proved particularly efficient in the attacks which they made at various times, but it must not be forgotten that, although their Japanese counterparts were more effective, their colleagues at air bases ashore had suffered extraordinary reverses. The twin-engined bombers of the 25th Japanese Naval Air Group, for instance, which had been relied on to wreak havoc among the Allied vessels, had no success whatever and even suffered a large number of losses.

The Japanese pilots of this group did not have the pluck, the perseverance or the pig-headedness which had characterised them when their bombers attacked the British warships *Prince of Wales* and *Repulse* in the Malay Archipelago on December 10, 1941. They attacked Admiral Crace's ships, which were manned by well-trained crews determined to defend themselves, and were driven off without having even touched the target. Was this result due to the deficiencies of the Japanese pilots or to the effects of the Allied anti-aircraft fire to which the sailors concerned were quite unaccustomed? We incline to the latter theory in view of the fact that the Americans and their allies were always ready to draw lessons from earlier defeats.

In conclusion, we may say that the Japanese plans for Operation *MO* were well thought out, although very complicated, and that they might have resulted in victory having regard to the political and military situation obtaining at that time, and also the number of ships engaged. They depended on the enemy's behaving in the way the Japanese had predicted. As soon as the Americans took an unforeseen initiative or varied the order of the actions they were expected to make, Japanese plans and decisions began to topple, seeming to lack any alternative measures in case of emergency. This was to prove an almost pathological weakness on the part of the Japanese, and was due in our opinion to their congenital inability to adapt quickly to the ever-changing conditions of battle. In this way they were the diametrically opposite of the Americans who were on many occasions to wring tactical advantages from them.

The battle of the Coral Sea is a perfect example of this psychological phenomenon. Had the Allies kept to the courses, the timetables and the actions which the Japanese had 'assigned' to them, there is no doubt that Operation *MO* would have probably been successful. They were confronted however, by the dynamic Fletcher, together with the liberal administration which was characteristic of the Americans. The same psychological handicap was found on many occasions during hostilities in the Pacific; one might even say that in almost all the later engagements, the Japanese defeats were due more to this intangible characteristic than to purely military factors.

Finally, the reproach incurred by Inoue of not having followed up the consequences of the presence of Crace's ships south of the Jomard Passage and the loss of the aircraft carrier *Shoho*, both quite insignificant errors in themselves, may perhaps be explained by the fact that this admiral had no special knowledge of the problems concerning aircraft. In this respect Takagi was similarly placed, since, except for Hara, he had no officer on his staff with experience of aircraft. This basic point refutes the argument that the Japanese could have exploited their tactical success and perhaps even sunk the *Yorktown* by launching a second attack. Inoue and Takagi were sailors and confined themselves to reporting the only losses they were told about and the damage inflicted on their adversaries, and on this basis considered it wise to retire. Again, would it have been possible, as Admiral Yamamoto claimed, to launch a second attack with the *Zuikaku* alone, which, although intact, was left in the afternoon of May 8 with only 24 *Zero* fighters, nine *Val* dive-bombers and six *Kate* torpedo aircraft? It is quite true that this battle represented a serious loss of aircraft for the Japanese, but the loss of so many highly trained pilots was even worse. This problem was so serious that, when the *Zuikaku* returned to Japan, it was much easier to replace her aircraft than the pilots which had been lost. It was for this reason that the *Zuikaku* did not take part in the great confrontation off Midway. From this it would appear that, quite apart from its strategic consequences and its immediate psychological effects, the battle of the

Top: This Kawanishi 97 H6K4 (*Mavis*) enveloped in flames and about to sink a short distance away from the American fleet. The Japanese aircrew however had sufficient time to warn Admiral Inoue.

Above: The Japanese tactical aircraft carrier *Zuikaku*, for which the battle of the Coral Sea proved to be her last engagement.

Above: The US aircraft carrier *Lexington* photographed during the battle shortly before the Japanese attack.

Below: Hit by a Grumman F4F 3 Wildcat, a Kawanishi 97 H6K4 (*Mavis*) on fire and about to come down on to the sea and sink.

Above: Taken by surprise by American fighters guided for the first time by radar, this Japanese four-engine Kawanishi H6K4 (*Mavis*) on fire managed to come down on the water.

Below: The Japanese light aircraft carrier *Shoho* photographed shortly before the start of Operation *MO*.

These two photographs were taken in immediate succession and show an American TBD 1 Douglas Devastator releasing its torpedo against the Japanese light aircraft carrier *Shoho* already suffering from the effects of a bomb. In the second photograph, the missile explodes on the vessel's starboard beam, thus putting an end to her career.

Above: The US tanker *Neosho* was unable to withstand for long the successive waves of the Japanese attack and sank after several days adrift on the Coral Sea.

Below: The heavy cruiser USS *Portland* (commanded by Captain Perlman) provided effective defence for the aircraft carriers of Task Force 17, scoring several hits on the waves of Japanese aircraft attacking them.

Above left: Taken while Task Force 17 was advancing in the Coral Sea, this photograph shows SBD 2 Douglas Dauntless dive-bombers on the flight deck of the US aircraft carrier *Lexington* with the USS *Yorktown* in the background.

Left: The US heavy cruiser *Chicago* which, commanded by Captain Bode, formed part of the naval force assigned to the British Rear-Admiral Crace, which blocked the Jomard Passage.

Above: Rear-Admiral Aubrey W. Fitch was, from on board the USS *Lexington*, in overall command both of the group of US aircraft carriers and of all air operations during the battle.

Right: The heavy US cruiser *Astoria* (under Captain Scanland) which, like others of her class, provided AA defence for the aircraft carriers of Task Force 17.

Rear-Admiral Frank J. Fletcher was in command of Task Force 17, from his HQ aboard the US aircraft carrier *Yorktown*. His bold decisions failed in some cases to be appreciated by his superior officer, Admiral Nimitz.

Rear-Admiral Thomas C. Kinkaid in command of the 5 heavy cruisers in the attacking group of Task Force 17 subject to orders from Rear-Admiral Frank J. Fletcher.

Coral Sea had a not insignificant effect on the Midway action which was to restore the political and military balance of the conflict.

A new type of battle

But these were not the only lessons to be learnt from this battle; a new factor was now present. This factor was due to the force of events, but was nonetheless highly significant and premonitory. This was the first time in the history of naval warfare that two hostile fleets had joined battle without once catching sight of each other, or exchanging gunfire. Everything took place remotely and via the agency of aircraft.

This was the first battle to take place 'below the horizon' and the first in which air groups on both sides assumed the rôle of long-range guns. By increasing the distances between opposing fleets, this new factor was to establish both the active and passive reconnaissance carried out by carrier aircraft as the main feature of future naval engagements. At the same time it once and for all removed the battleship from the pedestal it occupied as the capital ship of the battle squadrons.

The battle of the Coral Sea thus had the strategic effect of promoting the aircraft carrier to senior rank among fighting ships and of increasing its numbers. From this time on more ships of this type were built and anti-aircraft defence was increased along with the effective strength of the air squadrons embarked. Although it was not the signal for the disappearance of short-range naval actions, it was nevertheless the fore-runner of the great battles of the future which were to follow a similar pattern.

Throughout the world, the detractors of the aircraft carrier as the capital ship of a naval force maintained that this type of ship was too costly and also presented a target which was particularly tempting and vulnerable owing to its size and the considerable reserves of fuel and bombs which it carried. They were obliged to accept that the *Yorktown* and the *Lexington* had received numerous severe blows without immediately sinking, despite their 'congenital vulnerability'. The same applied incidentally to the Japanese vessel *Shokaku*. It had to be assumed that the subsequent loss of the *Lexington* was much more due to carelessness or to the inadequate protection or security provided by her aircraft than to the immediate effect of the blows she had received. For instance, without the spark from one auxiliary electric motor, the petrol vapour would never have caught fire and the great aircraft carrier would doubtless have reached a dockyard where repairs would have made her fit for subsequent operations.

In the United States, the announcement of the orderly abandonment of the 'Lady Lex', which had been accomplished, as we know, with discipline, calm and safety, was so encouraging and so indicative of the morale of the Navy in general and her crew in particular, that it almost obscured the actual loss of the vessel. The Americans, who were always very quick to draw lessons from a situation, profited from this one by adding a number of useful modifications to the large number of aircraft carriers under construction.

Although geographically and strategically independent of the battle of Midway which was impending, the naval air engagement in the Coral Sea had a very significant effect. On the one hand, the experience it provided enabled the value and tactical yield of the American air groups, which were to achieve sensational results at Midway, to be improved, but the battle of the Coral Sea deprived the Japanese of two of their most recent aircraft carriers which were therefore unable to take any part in the Midway action. The *Shokaku* was not available, owing to the damage she had received, and the *Zuikaku*, although intact, was not immediately operational owing to her extensive aircraft losses.

In the light of the direct and indirect lessons of this naval-air confrontation, the battle of the Coral Sea can be said to have a historical importance which has not always been recognised. It marked (a) the first halt in the Japanese military offensive, (b) the first engagement 'below the horizon', (c) the use of the aircraft carrier as the main vessel of a fleet, (d) the first awareness in America that all was not yet lost, and it was also the prototype of a series of naval air battles which would untimately enable the Allied forces to regain their supremacy throughout the Pacific.

CHAPTER FOUR

An analysis of equipment and technology

A decisive field

As mentioned in the introduction, it may be useful and even essential to discuss the technical aspect of the battle. Modern warfare (of which the Second World War may be considered as the first of this type) relies so much on technological data, that is to say on the military equipment used, that some time should be devoted to this subject. There is no need to deal with this secondary aspect at any length or in detail, but it would appear desirable to concentrate on certain principles for the benefit of less experienced readers. For instance, the Second World War showed, as early as 1939 in Poland, that war equipment plays a very great part in the course and outcome of modern conflicts. Such equipment cannot of course take the place of strategy nor of individual bravery, but it complements both of these and also their fields of application.

During this narrative, a certain number of specific types of equipment have only been referred to by their official names, and an author cannot dilate upon such terms without destroying or even prejudicing the clarity and continuity of his text. For this reason it is necessary to insert at this point a few brief technicalities designed to familiarise the readers with the properties of each type of equipment used.

Subsequent conflicts (and there have been a good few of these since 1945) have proved that technical progress has never ceased. Thus, man has become more and more the instrument of his own creations. One cannot go so far as to say that the modern soldier has become 'the sorcerer's apprentice, caught up in his own magic', but it is true that, quite apart from his human qualities, he is steadily becoming the slave of this own weapons.

During the Second World War, certain actions were obviously futile when carried out, however courageously, against the clearly superior quality and quantity of technical equipment. Everyone has at some time sensed the stupidity, for example, of cavalry charges against armoured units, or of swords used in the face of a machine gun. The same applies, perhaps even to a larger extent, to the field of naval air engagements to which the battle of the Coral Sea belongs.

From this point of view, the material power on both sides was evenly distributed in this battle, at least so far as air power was concerned, and this is perhaps why this chapter is important, since the tactical situations which developed depended at times only on particular technical information regarding the 'hardware' used by both parties.

The war in the Pacific, which was the archetype of war to the death between naval air groups, led both sides to employ aircraft carriers as the ideal bases for aircraft. This principle resulted, as we have seen, in a new type of fighting force, but it was also a stimulus to remarkable progress in the aeronautical field. We shall thus begin our brief study of the equipment involved by considering the aircraft involved.

It was during the period between the wars that the foundations were laid for what was to develop into the carrying of aircraft on board special carriers. The various types of aircraft then in use formed the basis for the composition of air groups on board aircraft carriers, and three specific types of aircraft emerged, which were designed to extend the range and destructiveness of naval air power. The three types of aircraft concerned were fighters, dive-bombers and torpedo aircraft. The fighter had the natural rôle of intercepting enemy aircraft and defending a fleet at close range; the dive-bomber carried out the attack itself like a very long-range gun, and the torpedo aircraft, bearing one of the most formidable weapons in sea warfare, proved an effective method of shortening the distance at which torpedoes could be used and extending the range of surface torpedo vessels. This was why during the thirties most of the world's aircraft carriers carried what we might term a trio of combat aircraft.

As regards the war in the Pacific, the opposing sides had at their disposal a number of aircraft carriers which were all equipped with three standard types of aircraft. At the time when the battle of the Coral Sea took place, the Japanese trio consisted of the Mitsubishi A6M.2 Type 0 (*Zero*) single seater fighter, the two-seater Aichi 99 D3A.1 (*Val*) dive-bomber and the three-seater Nakajima 97 B5N.1 (*Kate*) torpedo aircraft. This last could also be used, after certain slight modifications, as a horizontal bomber at both bigh and medium altitudes.

On their side the Americans had the single-seater Grumman F4F.3 Wildcat fighter, the two-seater Douglas SBD.2–3 Dauntless dive-bomber and the three-seater Douglas TBD.1 Devastator torpedo aircraft, and it is interesting to discuss and compare these three types of aircraft as developed by each of the two nations involved.

Mitsubishi A6M *Zero*

This famous aircraft deserves some reference to its history. Not only was it the most well known and the most used of all the aircraft belonging to the Empire of the Rising Sun, but its design, its aerodynamic qualities and its length of life were quite extraordinary.

Indeed, this aircraft immediately involves us in the air policy pursued by the Japanese ever since the beginnings of military aviation. The Mitsubishi A6M *Zero* was a remarkable aircraft which was at once the symbol and the spearhead of Japanese air power during the first three years of the war in the Pacific. It had an ancestry, the roots of which go back far into the period of Japan's preparation for her vast military expansion.

Japanese air marshals and their staffs had realised even in the twenties the advantage to be gained from military aircraft, and they had put enormous industrial effort into equipping their country with a large airforce. To satisfy her many and obscure plans for establishing a hegemony, Japan adopted an offensive policy, that is to say the creation of an airforce whose main purpose was to attack. She also concentrated on performance. Everything was sacrificed to this aim, even the protection both of the pilots and the vital parts of the aircraft they flew. This policy led to the production of ultra-light aircraft with astonishing performances but also extreme flimsiness and vulnerability. This handicap was not of great significance, however, since firstly the tactical effect was expected to be overwhelming, and secondly the life of the individual soldier had never counted for very much in Japan.

The Mitsubishi A6M *Zero*[1] fighter was the outstanding example of Japan's air policy. When Jiro Horikoshi, who was chief engineer of the firm of Mitsubishi, designed this astonishing single-seater fighter,

1 It should be noted that the Japanese calendar is 660 years ahead of our era, so that AD 1940 corresponds to the year 2600 since the beginning of the Japanese recorded time. The date is expressed only by the two last figures, ie. 00, and more simply as 0. Hence the *Zero* added to the official designation.

no other interceptor in the world could be compared with it. Its speed, armament and above all its manoeuvrability made it the best of its type. The first series models had appeared in China and then, in 1940, during Japanese military movements in the northern part of French Indo-China. The Japanese pilots had learned to make full use of this aircraft's magnificent performance and were fully trained long before their surprise attack on the great naval base at Pearl Harbor on December 7, 1941. It was natural that the *Zero* fighter should take part in all the engagements in the Pacific, and they brought off numerous victories. The *Zeros* very soon established the reputation of a formidable and even invincible adversary, which went so far as to become a quasi-demoniacal cult. The aircraft's reputation was such that as soon as an Allied pilot caught sight of a Japanese single-seater fighter he nicknamed it *Zero* and immediately became terrified of it.

Of monocoque construction in two sections connected together by a bolted-on ring, the Mitsubishi A6M *Zero* was fitted with a 950hp Nakajima Sakae 12 engine and two 20mm guns mounted in the wings and two synchronised 7.7mm machine guns on the engine hood. As we said earlier, everything was sacrificed to performance. No protection was provided. The aircraft was constructed of an ultra-light alloy ESD produced by the firm of Sumitomo. Incredibly light for an interceptor of this type carried by aircraft carriers and equipped with such formidable weapons, the A6M *Zero* could not but be extraordinary. It was able to loop at relatively low altitudes (where no other fighter would dare to follow), was very fast in climbing, and had a very wide radius of operation. Thus, the Mitsubishi fighter very speedily acquired a reputation which was never surpassed.

During operations in the Pacific, the firm of Mitsubishi modified its product to a certain extent in order to increase its superiority. In particular the wing span was reduced to give Model 32 which in the meantime had also been given the new 1130hp Nakajima Sakae 21 engine. This advanced technology, which had made of the *Zero* an aircraft considerably ahead of its time, did not seem able or willing to keep up with the progress made by the Americans, who eventually produced aircraft which outdid the *Zero* fighter in both quality and quantity.

During the year 1944, Model 52 appeared, but was unable to restore the technological balance which was tilting increasingly in

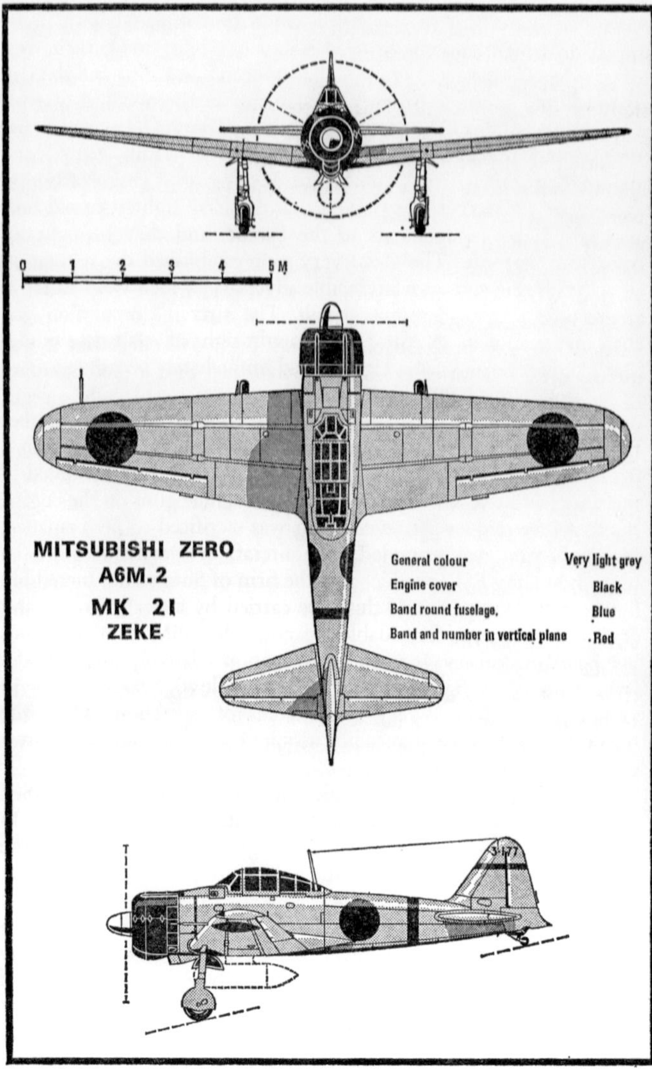
0 1 2 3 4 5 M
MITSUBISHI ZERO
A6M.2
MK 21
ZEKE
General colour Very light grey
Engine cover Black
Band round fuselage. Blue
Band and number in vertical plane Red
3-177

favour of the Allied fighters. In the last few months of the war numerous variants were produced. These were mainly characterised by an appreciable increase in the number of weapons carried and the transport of a 500lb bomb. This was the type of *Zero* which shared in, and to some extent gave a lead to, the Kamikaze suicide attacks.

During 1942 the firm of Nakajima, who also produced the A6M aircraft under licence, marketed a seaplane version, a few of which were used at bases on the islands. Its results were not good however, mainly owing to the appreciable reduction in performance due to the presence of the floats. Finally, two two-seater advanced training versions were produced by subsidiary companies.

The irrefutable superiority of the *Zero* fighter during the first two years of the war in the Pacific has not been overrated, but it was increased by a factor of at least ten by the fact that at the beginning of hostilities the Allied Powers had in the Far East only aircraft which were mostly obsolescent. Moreover, the Japanese military leaders had concentrated on the need to train pilots to a level at which they had perfect mastery over their aircraft. This problem was, incidentally, to become critical for Japan after the excellent pilots she had had at the beginning of the war had been shot down and could not be replaced except by hastily trained pilots who no longer possessed the admirable qualities of their courageous colleagues.

The Mitsubishi A6M fighter was none the less a remarkable aircraft and its name will for ever be linked with the great Japanese military offensive of the years 1941–1942. It will also remain for all time a significant element in the history of aviation. To illustrate the technical improvements introduced into the single-seater Mitsubishi A6M during the war, the characteristics and performance of the two most famous and most active versions of the aircraft are appended.

One final enormous explosion from inside the great aircraft carrier USS *Lexington* before she disappears beneath the Coral Sea.

Above: This photograph was taken during the Japanese air attack on the aircraft carrier USS *Lexington*. Already damaged, the aircraft carrier is about to be struck afresh by a torpedo aircraft Nakajima 97 B5N2 (*Kate*) flying very low.

Below: The three-seater Nakajima 97 B5N2 (*Kate*) had considerable aerodynamic properties, and it was this aircraft which was claimed to have destroyed the aircraft carrier *Lexington*.

Above: The remarkable performance record of the Mitsubishi A6M2 Zero (*Zeke*) gave it a formidable reputation even before the battle of the Coral Sea.

Below: Flown by highly trained crews, the Japanese dive-bomber Aichi 99 D3A2 (*Val*) was a formidable instrument of war.

Above: During the Japanese air attack, the gunners on board the American aircraft carrier *Yorktown* established a record for rapid and accurate fire and brought down several of their attackers.

Below: These SBD 2 Douglas Dauntless dive-bombers are getting ready to take off from the carrier USS *Yorktown* and attack Tulagi.

Above: The SBD 2 Douglas Dauntless dive-bomber was mainly responsible for American successes. Its accuracy, and therefore, its effectiveness, increased with the number of attacks it made.

Below: These three-seater TBD1 Douglas Devastator torpedo aircraft are returning to their own carrier after attacking the Japanese carriers. Unfortunately they had scored no hits.

6-T-11

41-F-8

Above left: A TBD 1 Douglas Devastator, a particularly slow and vulnerable type of aircraft, releasing its torpedo against a Japanese target.

Left: The single-seater carrier-based Grumman F4F 3 Wildcat represented an unsuccessful attempt to produce an aircraft which would outrival its Japanese counterpart the Mitsubishi A6M2 Zero (*Zeke*).

Above: Lieutenant Edward Henry 'Butch' O'Hare of the aircraft carrier USS *Lexington* showed outstanding bravery in handling his single-seater Grumman F4F 3 Wildcat.

Right: Captain Frederick C. Sherman, the energetic commander of the USS *Lexington*, was highly regarded by his crew, and his decisions were made under dramatic circumstances.

Above: The Japanese aircraft carrier *Shokaku* under attack from carrier-based American aircraft. The Japanese vessel easily evaded the American torpedoes which were faulty.

Below: Another photograph of the Japanese aircraft carrier *Shokaku*, taken just as a bomb from an SBD 3 Douglas Dauntless landed on her. The ship was damaged but was able to fight on and reach Japan.

Specification data relating to the Mitsubishi A6M Zero fighter

Technical Values	A6M.2 Version Model 21	A6M.5 Version Model 52
Wing span	12.00m	11.00m
Length	9.06m	9.12m
Height	3.51m	3.51m
Wing surface	22.44m²	21.30m²
Weight unloaded	1,680kg	1,867kg
Carrying capacity	730kg	857kg
Weight when loaded	2,410kg	2,733kg
Wing load	105kg/m²	128kg/m²
Power/weight ratio	2.50kg per hp	2.80kg per hp
Fuel capacity	518 litres (138 US gals)	570 litres (171 US gals)
Engine	Nakajima Sakae 12	Nakajima Sakae 21
Power	940hp	1,130hp
Propeller	3 bladed const. speed	3 bladed const. speed
Diameter	2.90m	3.05m
Maximum speed	331mph	350mph
Cruising speed	207mph	230mph
Climbing speed	18,000ft in 7 mins	18,000ft in 6 mins 8 secs
Landing speed	74.5mph	71.5mph
Ceiling	30,000ft	35,250ft
Range	1,470 miles	1,193 miles
Armament carried	2× 20mm cannons 2× 7.7mm machine guns + 250lb bomb	2× 20mm cannons 2× 7.7mm machine guns + 500lb bomb

Aichi 99 *Val*

Japanese aeronautical engineers had begun very early to design an aircraft which would carry an HE bomb and drop it on target with a very high degree of accuracy. This task was made more urgent by the requirements of the Japanese Navy, and it soon became clear that the best way of meeting these was to approach the target in a dive. To achieve this approach, it was necessary to design an aircraft powerful and solid enough to carry one or more bombs, and yet light enough to carry out the delivery dive without losing stability. Even in the thirties, several versions had been designed, some of which were used by aircraft carriers. The majority of these aircraft, however, did not reach the required standard, particularly the Japanese naval staff's desire for a monoplane – which would be the first of its kind.

At that moment the German firm of Junkers produced its first Stuka,[1] the famous Ju.87 which was designed with a wing undersurface to act as a brake during the dive. This property considerably reduced the aircraft's rate of dive without affecting its stability, thus ensuring great accuracy of aim. The Japanese were not slow to take advantage of this invention, and, basing their fuselage designs partly on the Ju.87's ability to retard diving speed and partly on the products of another German firm (Heinkel He66, He70 and He74), the firm of Aichi had by 1936 established a specifically naval type of two-seater aircraft, a low-wing monoplane constructed entirely of metal.

This Aichi model represented not only the latest development but also the best of its kind. It was called the D3A.1 Type 99[2] when its series production began. Although this bomber was fitted with a non-retractable undercarriage, just like the Ju.87, its speed and handling properties were such that, after launching its bombs, it could be used as a fighter. Although initially equipped with a Mitsubishi Kinsei 44 engine of 1075hp, it was later given the Kinsei 54 engine of 1300hp which increased its speed.

As soon as it appeared on the China front, the Allies code-named it *Val*. The Aichi 99 very soon established a reputation for being extremely suitable for the operations concerned, and the first Pacific engagements in which it took part proved how effective it was. A large number of Allied ships were lost as a result of its dive-bombing

[1] Abbreviation of *Stürzka*mpfflugzeug (=Dive-bomber) – Translator.

[2] '99' to indicate the Japanese calendar year 2599, ie. their equivalent of the Western 1939.

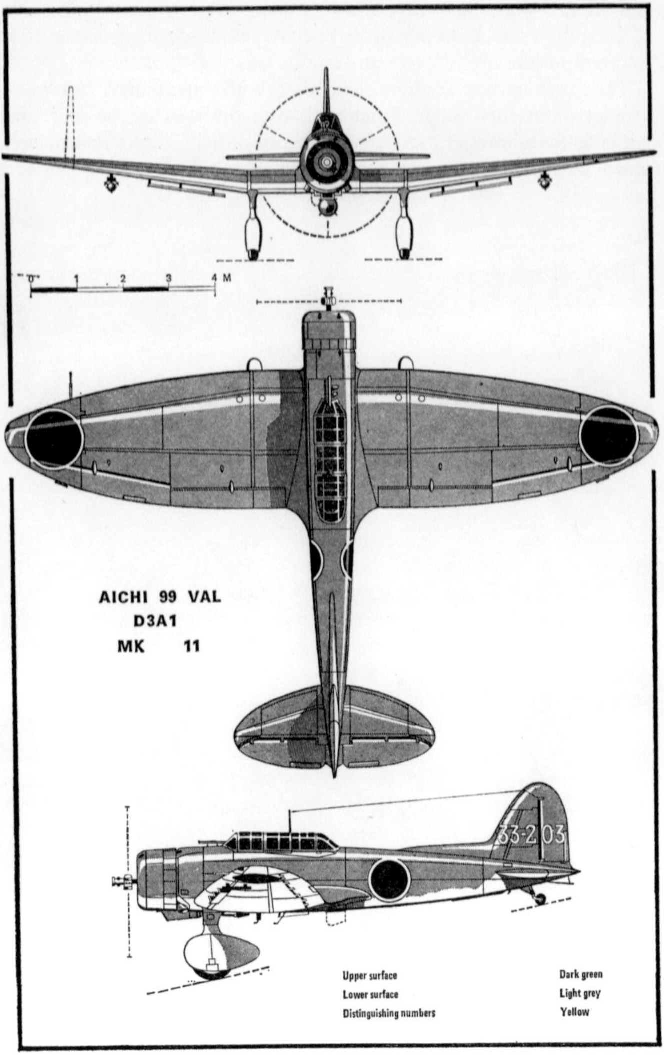
0 1 2 3 4 M
AICHI 99 VAL
D3A1
MK 11
33-203
Upper surface
Lower surface
Distinguishing numbers
Dark green
Light grey
Yellow

activities. It was able to dive at a very acute angle without losing any of its stability and, owing to its relatively low speed of descent, its pilot could literally 'deposit' his bombs on the target.

The Japanese war archives show that, with experienced and well-trained pilots such as the Japanese had at the start of the war, the Aichi 99 dive-bomber established a record of 80% direct hits, which was – and still is – unsurpassed in this field.

Technical specification relating to the Aichi 99 Val

Wing span	14.364m
Length	10.231m
Height	3.348m
Wing surface	34.90m²
Wing load	108.5kg/m²
Power/weight ratio	3.46kg per hp
Weight unloaded	2,570kg
Carrying capacity	1,230kg
Weight when loaded	3,800kg
Fuel capacity	1,080 litres (290 US gallons)
Oil capacity	60 litres (15.8 US gallons)
Engine	Mitsubishi Kinsei 54
Power	1,300hp
Propeller	3 bladed
Diameter	3.20m
Maximum speed	267mph at 18,300ft
Cruising speed	183mph at 9,000ft
Landing speed	78mph
Climbing speed	9,000ft in 5 minutes
Ceiling	31,500ft
Range	930 miles
Crew	2 men
Armament	2× rigidly mounted 7.7mm machine guns 1 movable 7.7mm machine gun 1× 500lb bomb + 2× 120lb bombs or 4× 120lb bombs

Nakajima 97 B5N *Kate*

The torpedo has always been recognised as the most effective weapon at sea and experts throughout the world have sought to extend its applications. As soon as aircraft proved themselves capable of transporting a payload equal to the weight of a torpedo, a race began to produce a type which would extend the range of these missiles by carrying them as near to the target as possible. Thus the torpedo-carrying aircraft was born.

In Japan, various aeronautical engineers attempted to solve this difficult problem, and during the thirties the Japanese Naval High Command produced specifications with the idea of co-ordinating the wide range of experience acquired. Several aircraft manufacturers competed in this field until the firm of Nakajima produced the B5N.1 Type 97[1] monoplane to replace the ancient biplanes in current use.

This was the first monoplane of its class, and it also had a fully retractable undercarriage. Moreover it was constructed entirely of metal, which also set it apart from even the most up-to-date aircraft possessed by any nation. Its fuselage was slender and had been lengthened to give room for a three-seater, glass-covered cockpit together with a lavish wing spread. The B5N *Kate* soon established the reputation of being a 'good sailor' possessing excellent stability in flight. It was one of the first aircraft in the world to be fitted with Fowler-type flaps.

The Japanese military staff had requested the constructors to exploit the new aircraft's considerable and effective payload by developing its speed, stability and carrying capacity. In this respect the Japanese remained faithful to the principle of bombing during horizontal flight even where naval targets were concerned. It should be remembered that the Japanese had long been studying and experimenting with this type of attack, in which they had developed a high degree of efficiency.

The firm of Nakajima therefore designed the aircraft for two types of use, (i) for bombing horizontally at high and medium altitude with six bombs attached outside the aircraft, and (ii) for low-level torpedo attacks carrying a self-propelled torpedo weighing 1,600lb. In both these applications the B5N Type 97 produced excellent results, the best of which was their attack on Pearl Harbor where the two uses were rewarded with equal success and a great tactical victory.

[1] The year 2597 in the Japanese calendar, ie. 1937 in the West.

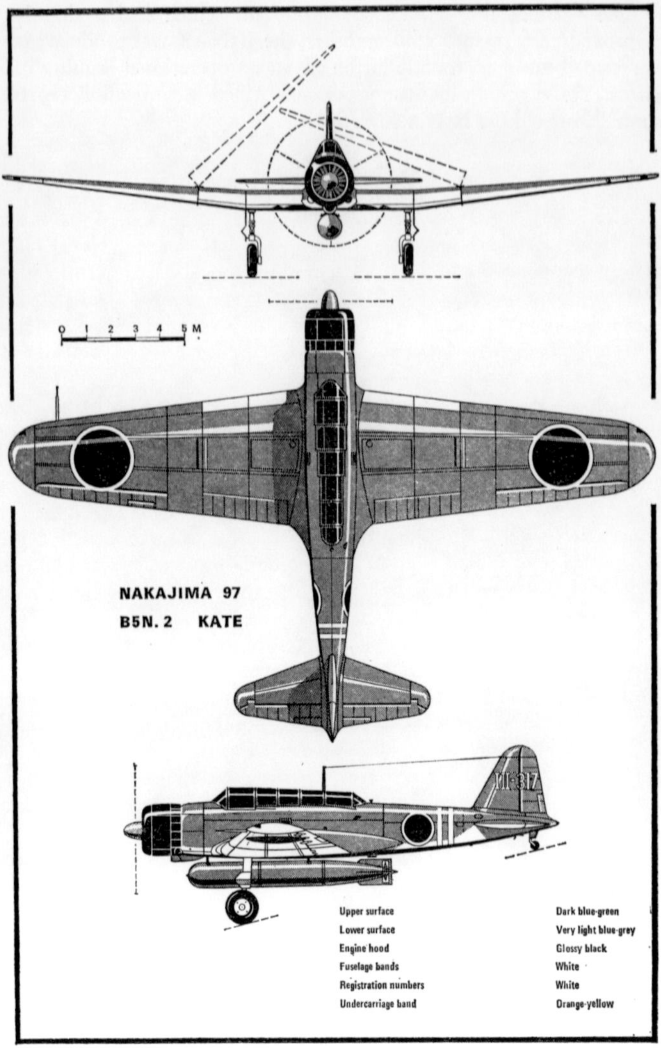
0 1 2 3 4 5 M
NAKAJIMA 97
B5N. 2 KATE
III-317
Upper surface
Dark blue-green
Lower surface
Very light blue-grey
Engine hood
Glossy black
Fuselage bands
White
Registration numbers
White
Undercarriage band
Orange-yellow

One version, the B5N.2 was produced, which had a slightly improved performance while another, the B5N.1K was produced in very small numbers for use in the advanced operational training of pilots. Those responsible for producing Allied identification charts soon christened the B5N.2 *Kate*.

Specification and performance of the Nakajima 97 B5N.2 Kate

Wing span	15.518m
Length	10.340m
Height	3.800m
Wing surface	$37.7m^2$
Wing load	$100.8kg/m^2$
Power/weight ratio	3.92kg per hp
Weight unloaded	2,279kg
Payload	1,521kg
Weight when loaded	3,800kg
Maximum weight	4,100kg
Fuel capacity	1,150 litres (304 US gallons)
Engine	Nakajima Sakae 11
Power	1,000hp
Propeller	3 bladed variable pitch
Diameter	3.20m
Maximum speed	235mph at 11,000ft
Cruising speed	163mph at 9,000ft
Landing speed	70mph
Climbing speed	9,000ft in 7 minutes 20 seconds
Ceiling	23,000ft
Range	634 miles
Crew	3 men
Armament	1× 7.7mm movable machine gun 1 torpedo Type 96 weighing 1,600lb or 1× 1,000lb bomb or 2× 500lb bombs or 6× 120lb bombs

Grumman F4F Wildcat

After completing its first flight on September 2, 1937, the XF4F.2 prototype represented the peak of American achievements in the production of carrier-based aircraft. This aircraft had descended from a long line of biplanes by the same makers and still retained many of its progenitors' characteristics in method of production, overall shape, retractable undercarriage, etc. A large series of Grumman F4F Wildcats was ordered in 1939, and these aircraft were the first interceptor monoplanes to be used by United States Navy aircraft carriers. This was in 1940.

Although its performance was comparatively poor, the F4F had the advantages of solidity and a fairly high degree of protection. At the end of the thirties, the establishments of the United States Navy, which were responsible for equipment, regarded Japanese aircraft with contempt, believing that the F4F fighter would suffice to cope with them. No attempt was therefore made to develop a more effective model, since it was generally thought that the existing fighter would wipe out the enemy on the other side of the Pacific in the event of hostilities.

Thus, when war broke out in the Pacific and the Grumman F4F Wildcats confronted the faster and more agile *Zeros*, the American pilots were at once both astounded and bitterly disillusioned. Efforts were made to improve the F4F, but it was impossible to reach the standard set by the Japanese in this field. It was not until the end of 1943, after two years of war, that a more competitive model could be set against the almost invincible *Zero*.

Meanwhile, a large number of Wildcats had been produced and took part in all the naval-air engagements during these first two years of hostilities. Since the Wildcat was inferior in almost every respect to the *Zero*, its pilots had no hope of scoring a victory unless they were very experienced and had the advantage of height. The standard of courage among these pilots was therefore a very high one. We need cite only two instances: Lieutenant 'Butch' O'Hare from the aircraft carrier *Lexington* and Captain 'Joe' Foss of Wing VMF121 of the Marines. Both these men achieved a fair number of victories often under very difficult conditions.

The production of the Wildcat, which was passed to the Eastern Aircraft Division of General Motors, still continued, the F4F being rejuvenated in a new form, viz. the FM.2 which took part in the battle of Leyte in October 1944, when it was embarked in the small

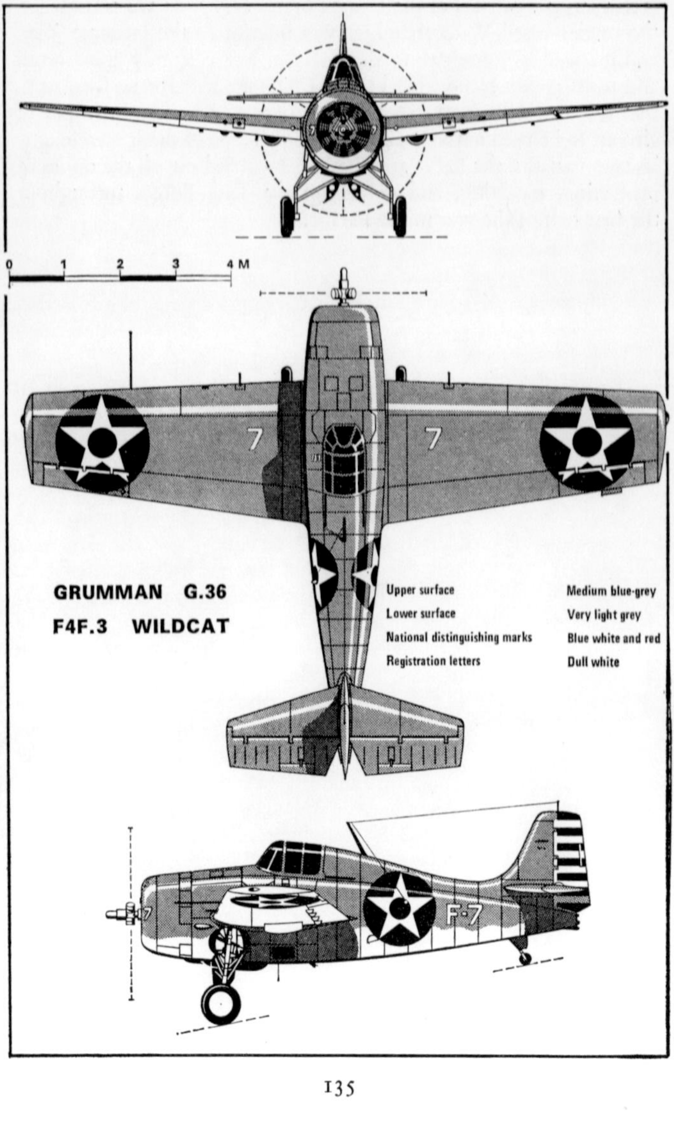
0 1 2 3 4 M
7
7
GRUMMAN G.36
F4F.3 WILDCAT
Upper surface
Medium blue-grey
Lower surface
Very light grey
National distinguishing marks
Blue white and red
Registration letters
Dull white
F-7

escort aircraft carriers of the United States Navy. As we said earlier, the carrier-based Wildcat fighter was inferior to the Japanese *Zero*, and it owed its longevity to the fact that it was stoutly constructed and to its ability to take hard knocks. Despite its poor performance, the Wildcat will always remain one of the most famous types of aircraft to be used in the Pacific, and some 8,000 of them were made. Its two variants, the F4F.3 and the F4F.4, carried out all the duties of protecting, escorting, and defending the Task Forces throughout the first half of the war in the Pacific.

Characteristics and performance of the Grumman F4F.3 Wildcat

Wing span	11.58m
Length	8.76m
Height	3.60m
Wing surface	24.154m²
Weight unloaded	2,425kg
Weight when loaded	3,179kg
Maximum weight	3,700kg
Engine	Wright R.1830–76
Power	1,200hp
Propeller	3 bladed Curtiss-Wright, const. speed
Maximum speed	329mph at 19,200ft
Cruising speed	147mph
Climbing speed	2,000ft per minute
Ceiling	34,300ft
Normal range	844 miles
Maximum range	1,689 miles
Armament	4× 12.7mm machine guns + bombs totalling 200lb

Douglas SBD Dauntless

Developed by Messrs. Northrop from the BT.2, the prototype Douglas XSBD.1 appeared at the beginning of 1939 and very soon revealed excellent qualities. Large numbers were ordered for series production and it became the standard American naval dive-bomber. It was relatively small for an aircraft of this type and proved very easy to handle. It was also able to carry a relatively large number of bombs, was heavily armed and turned out to have a very high degree of stability throughout its diving trajectory. This last was of course the main property required of a dive-bomber in order to achieve maximum accuracy.

To minimise its rate of descent and thus enable the trajectory to be corrected, the Dauntless was fitted with dive brakes. These took the form of perforated flaps which set up large air turbulences, thus enabling the pilot to aim with accuracy. From its very first engagement, the Dauntless showed its mettle and produced excellent results, particularly in the battles of the Coral Sea and Midway. It could be used as an attacking aircraft carrying a 900lb bomb or as a reconnaissance aircraft armed with a 450lb bomb. Like most dive-bombers, the Dauntless was fitted with a forked sling, designed to keep the centre bomb outside the sweep of the propeller immediately prior to release.

As mentioned above, the Douglas SBD Dauntless was very easy to handle for an aircraft of this class, as was proved on many occasions when a Dauntless, relieved of the weight of its bombs, would take on the rôle of a fighter and engage Japanese aircraft of this type. Again, the Dauntless was astonishingly long-lived for an aircraft used in this way. Like most American aircraft it was very solid and wore well. In the opinion of American naval pilots, the Dauntless was superior to later models introduced into the United States Navy, and those who flew it repeatedly praised its diving stability and its manoeuvrability, whilst deploring its slowness during horizontal flight.

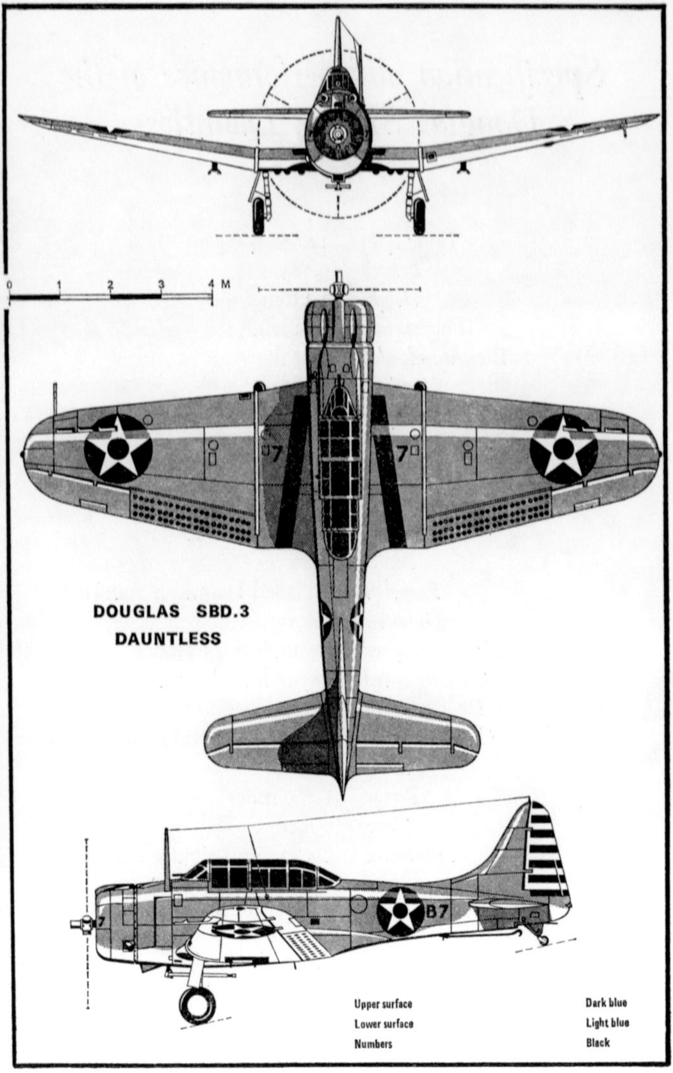
0 1 2 3 4 M
DOUGLAS SBD.3
DAUNTLESS
7
7
B7
Upper surface
Lower surface
Numbers
Dark blue
Light blue
Black

Specification and performance of the Douglas SBD.3 Dauntless

Wing span	12.652m
Length	9.785m
Height	4.140m
Wing surface	30.192m²
Weight unloaded	2,082kg
Payload	1,248kg
Weight when loaded	3,330kg
Maximum weight	4,050kg
Fuel capacity	982 litres (259.5 US gallons)
Oil capacity	59 litres (15.5 US gallons)
Engine	Wright R.1820–52
Power	1,000hp
Propeller	3 bladed Hamilton Standard
Diameter	3.276m
Maximum speed	246mph at 15,750ft
Cruising speed	185mph at 14,700ft
Landing speed	74mph
Climbing speed	9,00ft in 6 minutes 40 seconds
Ceiling	22,300ft
Range	1,100 miles
Crew	2 men
Armament	2× 12.7mm rigidly mounted machine guns 2× 7.7mm movable machine guns 1× 900lb bomb 2× 90lb bombs

Douglas TBD.1 Devastator

The Douglas Devastator was ordered in 1934, as a successor to a long series of biplane torpedo carriers and it made its first appearance in 1935. Not only was it the first monoplane torpedo carrier; it was also the first to be constructed entirely of light metal. This three-seater aircraft was based on a very conventional design, being given a generous wing spread and a semi-retractable undercarriage, ie. its wheels were only half buried in the thickness of the wing when retraction was complete.

The Devastator was taken into service in 1937 and on the outbreak of hostilities in the Pacific it was already the standard torpedo aircraft embarked in United States aircraft carriers. From the very beginning, however, the Devastator proved too slow and too vulnerable and became easy prey to the Japanese. The losses sustained in the battle of the Coral Sea, followed by the disastrous ones sustained off Midway, finally put an end to the Devastator's career. Its torpedoes were faulty, its speed was inadequate and its protection was ineffective, and so, despite the great courage of the men flying them, these aircraft inevitably suffered severely. To be certain of getting within effective range of its target, each Devastator would have needed at least one escorting fighter. To pose any threat to the enemy, it would have been necessary to persuade all their torpedoes to function. This of course could not be done.

The Devastator had its origin in an already obsolescent design and had none of the qualities required of a modern torpedo carrier. That is the real explanation of American failures in aircraft torpedo attacks throughout the first year of the war in the Pacific.

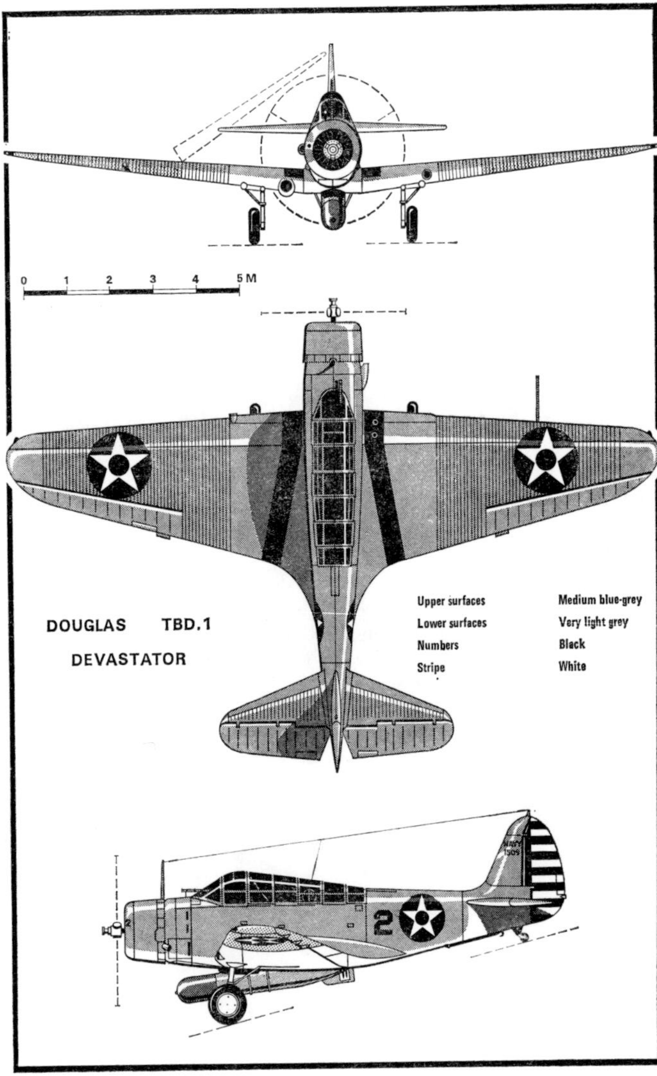
0 1 2 3 4 5 M
DOUGLAS TBD.1
DEVASTATOR
Upper surfaces Medium blue-grey
Lower surfaces Very light grey
Numbers Black
Stripe White
NAVY
1509
2

Specification and performance of the Douglas TBD.1 Devastator

Wing span	15.24m
Length	10.67m
Height	4.61m
Wing surface	39.2m^2
Weight unloaded	2,804kg
Weight when loaded	4,480kg
Maximum weight	4,624kg
Fuel capacity	818 litres (216 US gallons)
Engine	Pratt and Whitney R.1830–64
Power	900hp
Propeller	3 bladed, metal
Maximum speed	205mph at 7,500ft
Cruising speed	128mph
Landing speed	66mph
Climbing speed	700ft per minute
Ceiling	18,000ft
Range	652 miles
Crew	3 men
Armament	1× 7.7m rigidly mounted machine gun 1× 7.7mm movable machine gun 1× Bliss-Leavitt torpedo, 4.57m in length or 1× 900lb bomb

Kawanishi 97 H6K *Mavis*

Certain other types of aircraft were used by each side during the battle of the Coral Sea, but they played a much less decisive part in the war than the three types of carrier-based aircraft.

It would be unfair, however, not to mention the work of the reconnaissance aircraft, without which a carrier's aircraft would often have been unable to function. The Allies had no particularly outstanding aircraft of this type. This was due to the very minor, if not actually zero rôle assigned to reconnaissance by the Americans. The Japanese, on the other hand, made great use of large four-engined ocean-going seaplanes, a type of aircraft which is especially suitable for reconnaissance.

Japan was considerably interested in aviation, and very quickly developed all its aspects for military purposes. As a mainly maritime nation, the Japanese were conscious of the need to establish links between the various islands of their country and its numerous island dependencies. In the same way, to maintain her sovereignty, it was necessary for Japan to have a number of aircraft able to fly between her bases, which were often far apart, and to be able to alight anywhere on the vast areas of sea which they covered. Japan therefore quickly established a considerable force of seaplanes.

In the course of time, the Japanese aircraft industry produced a vast number of seaplanes of all shapes and sizes. When the Japanese Navy began to prepare for the great military offensive, Japan had available a considerable naval strategic force comprising a large fleet of surface vessels, numerous aircraft carriers and an ocean-going reconnaissance force of aircraft able to range far ahead of the fleet. Not only had the air crews been particularly well trained in the recognition of possible targets and in long distance flying, they were also equipped with types of aircraft very well suited to this type of mission.

Of all the numerous aircraft taken into service during the thirties, the Kawanishi 97 H6K was the most used and consequently the most familiar. The prototype appeared in July 1936 after both design studies and studies comparing it with the cream of the world's aircraft, which had taken two years to complete. As usual, the Japanese designers had copied the most advanced international methods, adding to them improvements in line with the Japanese national character. This Kawanishi aircraft was adopted almost at once by the Imperial Navy and was given the name 'Ocean Reconnaissance

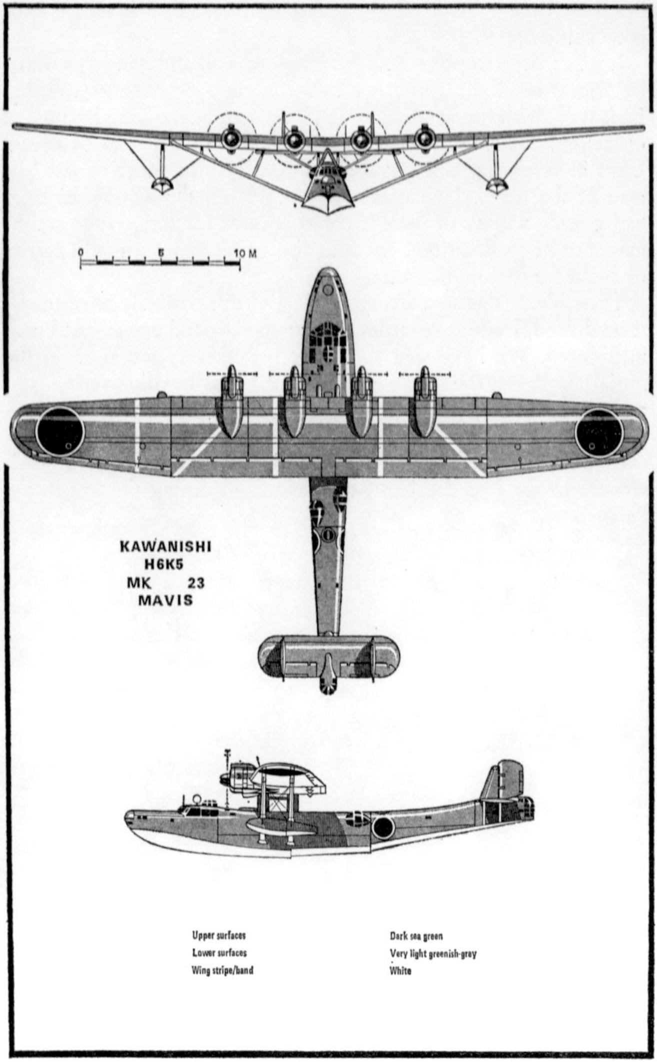
0 5 10 M
KAWANISHI
H6K5
MK 23
MAVIS
Upper surfaces
Dark sea green
Lower surfaces
Very light greenish-grey
Wing stripe/band
White

Seaplane Type 97' H6K.1, to which the Allies, a little later, gave the code name *Mavis*.

It was a large seaplane with parasol-type shell and wings, powered by four Mitsubishi Kinsei 43 radial engines developing 1,000hp. Endowed with great stability and an extremely long radius of operation, the H6K.1 was able to explore vast expanses of ocean. Used in every Japanese naval air base, it became more or less 'the eyes of the Fleet'. Like many large seaplanes, the Kawanishi H6K had a wide variety of uses. It could be used for long-range reconnaissance or explorations. It could also be used as a torpedo carrier or again for logistic purposes.

Throughout the next five years, 179 of these aircraft were made, several modifications regarding engine power and armament being introduced. We have seen the active part this aircraft took in the initial stages of the battle of the Coral Sea by discovering and reporting to the Japanese Naval Command the bearing and composition of Fletcher's Task Force 17. Although comparatively slow and rather vulnerable, the Kawanishi H6K rendered very great services to the Japanese Navy on every front during the war in the Pacific.

Specification and performance of the Kawanishi 97 H6K.5 Mavis

Wing span	40.00m
Length	25.63m
Height	6.27m
Wing surface	170.0m²
Wing load	103kg/m²
Power/weight ratio	3.65kg per hp
Weight unloaded	12,379kg
Weight when loaded	17,500kg
Maximum weight	23,000kg
Fuel capacity	13,414 litres (3,543 US gallons)
Engines	Mitsubishi Kinsei 53
Power	1,300hp
Propeller	3 bladed const. speed
Diameter	3.20m
Maximum speed	239mph
Cruising speed	161mph
Alighting speed on sea	66mph
Climbing speed	15,000ft in 13 minutes
Ceiling	28,800ft
Range	4,193 miles
Crew	9 men
Armament	1 movable 20mm cannon 4 movable 7.7m machine guns 2× 1,600lb torpedoes or 2× 1,000lb bombs

Technical lessons

In the light of this short comparative study of the aircraft used by both sides, it must be admitted that, in general, Japanese aircraft were rather lighter and swifter than their American counterparts. This lightness was achieved at the expense of an almost complete abandonment of protective shields in Japanese aircraft. Designed to take the offensive and to achieve optimum performance, they had only their speed and armament to depend on in avoiding battle and destroying or scattering their adversaries. This type of aircraft design held good as long as the Allies had only inferior equipment in the Far East. This was the case at the time of the battle of the Coral Sea, but thereafter the Japanese advantage gradually diminished, until the Americans, thanks to their more rapid technical advances, were well in the lead.

Another factor in the initial Japanese superiority in the air was the intensive training undergone by the pilots, which was also supplemented by operational experience in China. This was what gave Japan a supply of highly efficient, and operationally experienced air crews. It should also be noted that the Japanese carrier-borne aircraft of May 1942 were the first monoplanes in most of the aircraft categories involved.

It is, incidentally, astonishing that, in view of their superiority both in quality and quantity, the Japanese pilots did not inflict greater losses on the American carrier-based aircraft. Indeed, the opposite was rather the case. The reason for this unexpected balance of losses in the air was that, all in all, the aircraft of the American Navy were of tougher construction and were also fitted with armour which protected both the crew and the essential parts of the aircraft. It may therefore be said that, although inferior as regards performance, the United States Navy aircraft were able to take harder knocks without a corresponding loss of personnel. Neither, incidentally, did they catch fire immediately on impact, as happened to most of the Japanese aircraft.

It would therefore appear that there was a great fundamental difference in the air-war strategy pursued by each side. Without straying too far from the battle of the Coral Sea, it should be remembered that Japan maintained her policy right up until 1944 and that she only began to design aircraft with greater protection much too late to swing the balance of weapons in her favour and regain from the Allies the advantage that they had wrested from her in regard both to quality and quantity of aircraft.

The naval sphere

The naval air engagement in the Coral Sea was not confined solely to aircraft, and the ships opposing one another naturally played a great supporting rôle. The fact however remains that they never encountered one another directly, which is why this book could be sub-titled 'The Battle Below The Horizon', and, apart from the aircraft carriers, they took no direct part in the action. In view of this fundamental and definitive fact, it seems unnecessary to study the reciprocal qualities of the majority of the vessels present as we have done in the case of the aircraft involved.

Moreover, although the number of ships engaged were slightly different, the ships of neither fleet were really different in characteristics. The design and production of naval vessels on both sides were very similar and are therefore of no particular interest.

However, Admiral Takagi's two fighting aircraft carriers, the *Shokaku* and the *Zuikaku*, require some explanation in view of their having so recently been commissioned at the time of the battle. As we have seen, Japan was firmly committed to setting up a powerful naval air force, and, when plans for military expansion were laid, the Japanese Naval Command laid down the keels of a wide range of naval vessels.

This ambitious programme included both the *Shokaku* and the *Zuikaku*, which constituted a new generation of warships and were the fruit not only of experience gained through earlier ships, but also of the latest progress in aircraft equipment and anti-aircraft defence. Laid down during the second half of 1939, these two aircraft carriers were launched in 1941, only a short time before the start of hostilities in the Pacific.

The two vessels had a displacement of 25,675 tons, a length of 257 metres overall and were capable of a speed of 34 knots. They could carry 84 combat aircraft, a crew of 1,660 men and a minimum of 52 anti-aircraft guns ranging from 25mm to 127mm. Add to these brief characteristics the fact that the two ships were more up-to-date, longer and heavier than their most recent American counterparts (eg. the *Yorktown* and the *Enterprise*) and had a high maximum speed and outstanding naval qualities.

APPENDIX ONE

Table showing organisation and composition of the Japanese Naval and Air resources

Admiral Isoroku Yamamoto	Commander-in-Chief of Combined Fleet, on board the battleship *Yamato* anchored off Truk
Vice-Admiral Shigeyoshi Inoue	Commander-in-Chief of 4th Fleet as responsible for Operation *MO*, on board the cruiser *Kashima* anchored off Rabaul

MOBILE or STRIKING FORCE (Vice-Admiral Takeo Takagi)

5th Aircraft Carrier Division (Rear-Admiral Chuichi Hara)

2 vessels	*Zuikaku* (Admiral Hara's flagship) 72 aircraft
	Shokaku 72 aircraft

5th Cruiser Division

2 heavy cruisers	*Myoko* (Admiral Takagi's flagship)
	Haguro

Destroyer Flotilla

6 vessels	*Ariake*
	Yugure
	Shiratsuyu
	Shigure
	Ushio
	Akebono
1 fuel tanker	*Toho Maru*

LANDING FORCES (Rear-Admiral Aritomo Goto on board the heavy cruiser *Aoba*)

Tulagi Group (Rear-Admiral Kiyohide Shima)

1 mine-layer	*Okinishima* (flagship)
1 seaplane transport	*Kawa Maru*

22nd Destroyer Division

2 vessels	*Kikuzuki*
	Yuzuki
1 transport	*Asuman Maru*

+ various small supply vessels including the mine-sweeper *Tama Maru*

Port Moresby Group (Rear-Admiral Sadamichi Kajioka)

1 light cruiser (leader)	*Yubari* (flagship)
6 destroyers (which together with the cruiser made up the 6th Destroyer Flotilla)	*Oite*
	Asanagi
	Uzuki
	Mutsuki
	Yunagi
	Yahoi

11 ships carrying troops and equipment (Rear-Admiral Koso Abe)

+ various small supply vessels

Support Group, 18th Cruiser Division (Rear-Admiral Kuninori Marushige)

2 light cruisers	*Tenryu*
	Tatsuta
1 seaplane transport	*Kamikawa Maru*
3 gunboats	*Keijo Maru*
	Seikai Maru
	Nikkai Maru
1 mine-layer	*Tsugaru*

COVER FORCE (Rear-Admiral Aritomo Goto)

6th Cruiser Division

4 heavy cruisers	*Aoba* (flagship)
	Kako
	Kinugasa
	Furutaka
1 light aircraft carrier	*Shoho* 28 aircraft
1 destroyer	*Sazanami*
1 fuel tanker	*Hiro Maru*

LOOK-OUT FORCE (Captain Ishizaki)

Patrol Group

5 submarines	*I*.21, *I*.22, *I*.24, *I*.28, *I*.29

Raiding Group

2 submarines	*Ro*.33 and *Ro*.34

SHORE-BASED AIR SUPPORT

25th Air Group (Rear-Admiral Sadayoshi Yamada at Rabaul)

Rabaul Air Base (Yokohama Division)	44 A6M Mitsubishi *Zero* (fighters)
	41 G3M Mitsubishi *Nell* (bombers)
	13 H6K Kawanishi *Mavis* (reconnaissance)
Lae Air Base	16 A6M Mitsubishi *Zero* (fighters)
Buna Air Base	7 G3M Mitsubishi *Nell* (bombers)
Shortland Air Base	3 H6K Kawanishi *Mavis* (reconnaissance)
	4 light seaplanes
Tulagi Air Base (Tainan Squadron)	6 A6M.2N Nakajima *Zero* (fighters)

Deboyne Air Base	12 light reconnaissance seaplanes
Truk Air Base (reserve)	45 A6M Mitsubishi *Zero* (fighters)
	45 G3M Mitsubishi *Nell* (bombers)

Table of Japanese Air Groups

1ST AIR FLEET

Aircraft carrier *Shokaku*

Fighter Group	18	A6M.2 (*Zero*)
Bomber Group	27	99 D3A (*Val*)
Aerial Torpedo Group	27	97 B5N (*Kate*)
Grand total	72	
Available on May 8 (am)	60	
Available on May 8 (evening)	39	

Aircraft carrier *Zuikaku*

Fighter Group	18	A6M.2 (*Zero*)
Bomber Group (Commander Kakuichi Takahashi)	27	99 D3A (*Val*)
Aerial Torpedo Group (Commander Shigekazu Shimazaki)	27	97 B5N (*Kate*)
Grand total	72	
Available on May 8 (am)	61	
Available on May 8 (evening)	39	

Aircraft carrier *Shoho*

Fighter Group	16	A6M.2 (*Zero*)
Aerial Torpedo Group	12	97 B5N (*Kate*)
Grand total	28	
Available on May 7 (am)	21	
Available on May 7 (evening)	0	

APPENDIX TWO

Table showing organisation and composition of the American Naval and Air resources

Admiral Chester W. Nimitz	Commander-in-Chief of the Pacific Fleet (CINCPAC) at Pearl Harbor
Rear-Admiral Frank J. Fletcher	Commander-in-Chief of the naval and air forces engaged in the battle

TASK FORCE 17 (Rear-Admiral Frank Jack Fletcher)

Aircraft Carrier Group (Rear-Admiral Aubrey W. Fitch)

2 vessels	CV2 *Lexington* (Admiral Fitch's flagship) commanded by Captain Sherman: 71 aircraft
	CV5 *Yorktown* (Admiral Fletcher's flagship) commanded by Captain Buckmaster: 72 aircraft

Support Group (Rear-Admirals Thomas C. Kinkaid and W. W. Smith)

5 heavy-cruisers	CA27 *Chester* commanded by Captain Shock
	CA32 *New Orleans* commanded by Captain Good
	CA33 *Portland* commanded by Captain Perlman
	CA34 *Astoria* commanded by Captain Scanland

CA36 *Minneapolis* commanded by Captain Lowry

1st Destroyer Division (Captain Early)

4 vessels

DD349 *Dewey* commanded by Lt Cdr Chillingworth

DD354 *Monaghan* commanded by Lt Cdr Burford

DD355 *Aylwin* commanded by Lt Cdr Rogers

DD360 *Phelps* commanded by Lt Cdr Beck

Carrier-Escort Group

4 destroyers

DD411 *Anderson* commanded by Lt Cdr Ginder

DD412 *Hammann* commanded by Cdr True

DD414 *Russell* commanded by Lt Cdr Hartwig

DD417 *Morris* commanded by Cdr Jarrett

Logistics Group (Captain Phillips)

2 tankers

AO23 *Neosho* commanded by Captain Phillips

AO21 *Tippecanoe* commanded by Cdr Macondray

2 destroyers

DD352 *Worden* commanded by Lt Cdr Pogue

DD409 *Sims* commanded by Lt Cdr Hyman

SOUTH-WEST PACIFIC NAVAL FORCES (Vice-Admiral Herbert F. Leary)

Task Force 44 (Rear-Admiral J. C. Crace, Royal Navy)

2 heavy-cruisers

(Aust.) *Australia* (flagship) commanded by Captain Farncomb

	CA29 *Chicago* commanded by Captain Bode
1 light cruiser	(Aust.) *Hobart* commanded by Captain Howden

Destroyer Group (Commander MacInerney)

3 vessels	DD348 *Farragut* commanded by Lt Cdr Hunter
	DD377 *Perkins* commanded by Lt Cdr Ford
	DD416 *Walke* commanded by Lt Cdr Fraser

Salvage Group

2 destroyers	DD388 *Helm*
	DD391 *Henley*

Air Reconnaissance

Task Group TG17-9 (Commander de Baun)

1 seaplane replenisher	AV8 *Tangier* (based at Noumea)
2 reconnaissance squadrons VP71 and VP73	12 *PBY5* Consolidated Catalina

Look-out Group (Captain Christie)
Several patrolling submarines

Table of American Air Groups

Aircraft Carrier CV2 *Lexington* (2nd Air Group commanded by Commander W. B. Ault)

Squadron VF2 (commanded by Lt Cdr Ramsey)
23 Grumman F4F.3 Wildcat fighters

Squadron VB2 (commanded by Lt Cdr W. L. Hamilton)
18 Douglas Dauntless SBD.2–3 bombers

Squadron VS2 (commanded by Lt Cdr R. E. Dixon)
18 Douglas Dauntless SBD.2–3 bombers

Squadron VT2 (commanded by Lt Cdr Brett)
12 Douglas Devastator TBD.1 aerial-torpedo carriers

Total	71
Available at dawn on May 8	63

Aircraft Carrier CV5 *Yorktown* (5th Air Group commanded by Lt Cdr Pederson)

Squadron VF42 (commanded by Lt Cdr Fenton)
21 Grumman F4F.3 Wildcat fighters

Squadron VB5 (commanded by Lt Short)
19 Douglas Dauntless SBD.2–3 bombers

Squadron VS5 (commanded by Lt Cdr Burch)
19 Douglas Dauntless SBD.2–3 bombers

Squadron VT5 (commanded by Lt Cdr J. Taylor)

	13	Douglas Devastator TBD.1 aerial-torpedo carriers
Total	72	
Available at dawn on May 8	59	

APPENDIX THREE

OVERALL AMERICAN LOSSES

Naval Losses

Aircraft carrier *Lexington*	33,000 tons
Destroyer *Sims*	1,570 tons
Tanker *Neosho*	7,256 tons
	41,826 tons

Air Losses

Carrier aircraft	77

OVERALL JAPANESE LOSSES

Naval Losses

Light aircraft carrier *Shoho*	12,000 tons
Destroyer *Kikuzuki*	1,313 tons
Supply vessel *Okinoshima*	4,470 tons
3 mine-sweepers	850 tons
4 self-propelling lighters	
	19,000 tons approx.

Air Losses

Reconnaissance seaplanes	2
Twin-engine bombers	5
Single-engine seaplanes	3
Carrier aircraft	87
	97

Bibliography

Japanese references

Saburo Sakaī, Fred Saīto, Martin Caidin – *Samourai.*
Mitsuo Fuchida, Masatake Okumiya – *Midway, The Battle that Doomed Japan.*
Masatake Okumiya, Jiro Horikoshi, Martin Caidin – *Zero.*
Aireview – *The Fifty Years of Japanese Aviation 1910–1960.*
Aireview – *General View of Japanese Military Aircraft in Pacific War.*

American references

Samuel Elliot Morison – *History of United States Naval Operations in World War II.*
W. P. Puleston – *The Influence of Sea Power in World War II.*
John Toland – *But Not in Shame.*
E. B. Potter, Chester W. Nimitz – *The Great Sea War.*
Thaddeus Tuleja – *Climax at Midway.*
S. E. Smith – *The United States Navy in World War II.*
Louis Morton – *United States Army in World War II – The War in the Pacific – Strategy and Command – The First Two Years.*
Department of State – *The Army Air Force in World War II Volume One – Plans and Early Operations.*
Department of State – *An Abridged U.S. Naval Chronology of World War II.*

French references

Andrieu d'Albas – *Marine Imperiale.*
Albert Vulliez – *Tonnerre sur Le Pacifique.*

British references

Donald McIntyre – *The Battle for the Pacific.*

Gerald Bowman – *War in the Air.*
Courtney Browne – *Tojo, The Last Banzai.*
Paul H. Silverstone – *U.S. Warships of World War II.*
A. J. Watts – *Japanese Warships of World War II.*
R. J. Francillon – *Japanese Aircraft of the Pacific War.*
G. Swanborough, P. M. Bowers – *United States Navy Aircraft since 1911.*
F. G. Swanborough – *United States Military Aircraft since 1909.*

In addition, a very large number of operational reports, official statements and miscellaneous documents have been studied and compared.

Index

ABDA fleet 65
Abe R-Adm. 79
Afrika Korps 16
Aichi 99 D3A (*Val*) a/c 59; D3A.1 120–9 *passim*
*Air Group 2 89
Aleutian Islands 13, 21, 27
Allied Air Force Div. 55
Allies: counter-offensive 25; situation critical 69; losses 111
America's morale 111
American Forces: a/c carriers 19; Chiefs of Staff 21; Naval GHQ 22, 25; High Command 35; strategy 53; Task Force 68
amphibious operation 26
Anderson USS 102
Annapolis Naval Trng. Schl. 36
anti-aircraft: guns/gunfire 91, 97, 115; defences 94
Astoria USS 51
atmospheric conditions 67, 83, 89
Augusta class 66
Ault Cmdr. 69, 89, 91
Australia 18–35 *passim*, 109
Australia HMAS 63

Baker Ens. 75
Bali 13
'Batchelor's Button' 34
Batchelor Field 23
de Baun Cmdr. 53
Bismarck Arch. 34
blockade 26
Bomber Group 19th 55
Borneo 13, 32
Bougainville 26, 40–55 *passim*
Brett Capt. W. B. 89
Brett Lt. Gen. G. H. 55
Brisbane 23, 54, 108
Brown V-Adm. Wilson 22–3, 33
Buna 19, 52, 64
Burch Lt. Cmdr. 46, 87
Burma 13, 24
Buckmaster Capt. 33, 45, 96, 97

California class 66
Canberra 20
*Cape York 19
Caroline Islands 32
Catalina a/c 53, 108
Celebes Island 13
Chester USS 51
Chicago USS 35, 41, 45, 63
China 27
Christie Capt. 34
CINPAC (Pacific Fleet) 32
*Cloncurry 55
Coen 31
Congressional Medal of Honor 91
Cooktown 31
Coral Sea battle: conclusion 107; significance 108; Pyrrhic victory 111; 'battle of errors' 112
Corregidor 23, 57
Crace R-Adm. 33–116 *passim*
Curtin, John, P.M. Australia 20–1, 35, 109, 110

Darwin 23
Dauntless (Douglas) a/c 45–94 *passim*
Deboyne Island 30, 57, 70, 105
Devastator (Douglas) a/c 45–7, 70, 85–9

Dicken, Sig. 61
Dixon Lt. Cmdr. 70, 84, 85
Doolittle Lt. Col. 11, 27, 32
Douglas a/c (see Devastator and Dauntless) 121, 138, 140–1, 143
Duckworth Cmdr. 95
Dutch East Indies 20

East Indian Arch. 11
Eastern Asia 11, 12, 13
Ellice Islands 13, 21
Enterprise USS 21–2, 32, 35, 107
Entrecasteaux Islands 57
Espiritu Santo Island 34, 41
Europe 12

Far East 11, 12
Farragut USS 63, 65
Fiji Arch. 18, 21, 26
First World War 36
Fitch R-Adm. 33–101 *passim*
Fletcher R-Adm. 21–114 *passim*
Flights
- VB2 69, 88
- VB5 46
- VF2 89
- VF42 46, 88
- VS2 89
- VS5 46
- VT2 89
- VT5 46, 88

Flinders Capt. 28
Flying Fortress 23, 55
Forgy Lt. Cmdr. 102

Germany 21
Gilbert Islands 13, 21
Gilmour Cmdr. 97
Goto R-Adm. 30–57 *passim*, 68, 72, 85, 106, 112
Great Britain 12, 21
'Greater East Asian Co-prosperity Sphere' 13, 24, 38
Grumman (Wildcat) a/c 22, 45, 47, 121, 134, 136, 137
Guadalcanal 40, 50
Guam 13

Halsey V-Adm. 21–2, 33, 35
Hamilton Lt. Cmdr. 69, 70, 88
Hammann USS 50, 102
Hara R-Adm. 57–9, 74–88 *passim*, 92, 116
Hatton Lt. Col. 27
Hawaiian Arch. 12, 28
Healy Cmdr. 98, 99
Henley USS 108
Helm USS 108
Hideki, P.M. Japan 20
Hitler's telegram 109
Hobart USS 34, 63
Hornet USS 27, 32, 35, 107

Ichiu Hakko 15
India 16
Indian Arch. 13, 24, 32
Indo-Burmese border 13
Inoue V-Adm. 30–116 *passim*
Iro JS 53
Ishizaki Capt. 30

Jaulit Island 21
Japanese Forces: Air 58, 63, 67, 111, 112, 148; Army 19, 25, 25; High Command 24, 29, 38, 40, 68; Naval 17, 18, 30, 32, 34, 104, 111, 115, 149
Java 11, 13
Jomard Passage 30, 43, 52–7, 62–9, 72, 106, 114, 116

Kajioka R-Adm. 30, 40
Kamikawa Maru JS 57, 70
Kanno C.P.O. 80, 82
Kashima USS 37, 40
Kate (Nakajuma) a/c 60–97 *passim*, 116
Kavieng 21

Kawanishi (*Mavis*) a/c 144, 146, 147
Kikuzuki JS 46
King Adm. 35
Kincaid R-Adm. 102, 107
Kinugasa JS 59
Kwajalein Island 21

Lae 19, 23, 52
Leary V-Adm. 22–3, 33, 108
Lexington USS 22–117 *passim*; radar detects enemy 93; abandon ship 101; sinks 103
Louisiade Arch. 23, 29, 43–69 *passim*

MacArthur Gen. 23–54 *passim*, 63, 72, 85, 106, 113
Makambo 47
Malaita Island 51
Malaya 13, 24, 115
Manchuria 27
Marcus Island 22
Mavi (Kawanishi) a/c 52
Markin Island 21
Marshall Islands 21
Martin (Marauders) a/c 65
Marushige R-Adm. 30–68 *passim*, 112
Meloelap Island 21
meteorological information 44
Middle East 16
Midway 21–9, 104–18 *passim*
Mili Island 21
Minneapolis USS 102
Misima Island 30, 57, 67
Mitchell B25 a/c 51
Mitsubishi (*Zero*) a/c 59, 65, 120–5
Morris USS 100, 102
Myoko JS 79

Nakajima (*Kate*) a/c 59, 120, 130, 131, 133
Nauru Island 107
naval-air battles 118
Nell (Mitzubishi) a/c 65
Neosho USS 41–112 *passim*
Netherlands 12
New Britain 13
New Caledonia 18, 21, 26
New Guinea 13–32 *passim*, 73
New Hebrides 21, 34, 41
New Ireland 13
New Orleans 102
New Zealand 20
Nimitz Adm. 32–54 *passim*, 104, 107, 114
*North American B25 (Mitchell) a/c 27
North Queensland 31
Noumea Island 41, 108

Ocean Island 28, 107
O'Hare Lt. 22, 33
Okinoshima JS 107
Operation Midway 38
Operation *MO* 27–114 *passim*
Owen Stanley Mts. 19, 23

Pacific Ocean 11–51 *passim*, 120
Papua 23, 33
Pearl Harbor 11–36, *passim* 95, 107, 114
Pederson Lt. Cmdr. 46
Perkins USS 35, 41, 63
Peyton M/Sgt. 102
Phelps USS 102
Philippines 13, 24, 32
Phillips Capt. 61
Phoenix Islands 21
Poland 119
Port Moresby 19–73, 103–6 *passim*
Powers Lt. 83, 91
Prince of Wales HMS 64, 115
Puget Sound 32
'Purple' code 32

Rabaul 21–65 *passim*, 72, 106, 113
radar 51, 78, 82, 93, 112

reconnaissance a/c 43–54 *passim*, 80, 107
Renmell Island 53–4
Repulse HMS 64, 115
Rommel 16
Rossel Island 62, 72, 80
Russell USS 44–5
Russians 14
Rye USS 56

Salamaua 19, 23
Samoa Arch. 18, 21, 26
Saratoga USS 27, 32; 'S' class 103
Sazanami JS 70
'Scrub one flat-top' quot. 71
Second World War 119
Seligman Cmdr. 100, 102
Sherman Capt. 33, 92–102 *passim*
Shima R-Adm. 30, 40, 106–7
Shimazaki Capt. 96
Shoho JS 32–116 *passim*; sighted 69; sunk 70; symbolic loss 72; effect on Inoue 73
Shokaku JS 58, 80–103 *passim*, 117–18, 149
Short Lt. 46
Shortland Island 53
Sims USS 56–74 *passim*, 107, 112
Simpson Roadstead 37
Smith Lt. 84
Smith R-Adm. 50, 107
Solomon Islands 27–56 *passim*, 107
Soviet Union 16
Stalin 16
submarine S.42 107
Sumatra Island 13

Tagula Island 69
Takagi V-Adm. 30–116 *passim*, 149
Takahashi Lt. Cmdr. 59–80 *passim*
Tama Maru JS 46
Tangier USS 53
Task Forces 21, 22, 54
TF11 41, 52
TF17 40, 41, 44, 52–112 *passim*
TF44 33–64 *passim*
Taylor Lt. Cmdr. 46, 88
Thatch Lt. 33
Thursday Island 31
Timor 13
Tippecanoe USS 41
Tokyo 11, 20–2, 38, 111
Tomioka Capt. 25
Tongatebu 34, 107
*Torres Straits 19
Townsville 65, 81
Trojalkowski Cmdr. 97
Truk 31–2, 40, 106–7, 113
Tulagi Island 27–52 *passim*, 78, 107, 113–14

United States 11, 12, 117; Pacific Fleet 17; industrial potential 18; Navy 22; Navy Dept. 36

Val (Aichi) a/c 61, 74–5, 80, 93, 96, 116

Wainwright Gen. 57
Wake Island 13, 32
Walke USS 63
Warspite class 66
White Bay 37
Wildcat (Grumman) a/c 51–2, 75, 85–93 *passim*
Willis Islands 44
Wotje Islands 21

Yamada R-Adm. 30, 63–4
Yamamoto Adm. 17, 24–7, 103, 106, 113–14, 116
Yokohama JS 55
Yorktown USS 21–117 *passim*; manoeuvrability 97; Pearl Harbor 107; Midway 109
Yuzuki JS 47

Zero (Mitsubishi) a/c 55, 69–96 *passim*, 116
Zuikaku JS 56, 58, 82–118 *passim*, 149